Conversations with
Lenard D. Moore

Literary Conversations Series
Monika Gehlawat
General Editor

Conversations with
Lenard D. Moore

Edited by John Zheng

University Press of Mississippi / Jackson

The University Press of Mississippi is the scholarly publishing agency of
the Mississippi Institutions of Higher Learning: Alcorn State University,
Delta State University, Jackson State University, Mississippi State University,
Mississippi University for Women, Mississippi Valley State University,
University of Mississippi, and University of Southern Mississippi.

www.upress.state.ms.us

The University Press of Mississippi is a member
of the Association of University Presses.

Copyright © 2024 by University Press of Mississippi
All rights reserved
Manufactured in the United States of America
∞

Library of Congress Cataloging-in-Publication Data

Names: Zheng, Jianqing, editor.
Title: Conversations with Lenard D. Moore / John Zheng.
Other titles: Literary conversations series.
Description: Jackson : University Press of Mississippi, 2024. | Series: Literary
    conversations series | Includes bibliographical references and index.
Identifiers: LCCN 2024022960 (print) | LCCN 2024022961 (ebook) |
    ISBN 9781496853943 (hardback) | ISBN 9781496853950 (trade paperback) |
    ISBN 9781496853967 (epub) | ISBN 9781496853974 (epub) | ISBN 9781496853981 (pdf) |
    ISBN 9781496853998 (pdf)
Subjects: LCSH: Moore, Lenard D., 1958—Interviews. | African American
    poets—Interviews. | Poets, American—Interviews. | African American authors—
    Interviews. | American literature—African American authors—Interviews.
Classification: LCC PS3563.O6218 A5 2024 (print) | LCC PS3563.O6218 (ebook) |
    DDC 811/.54—dc23/eng/20240723
LC record available at https://lccn.loc.gov/2024022960
LC ebook record available at https://lccn.loc.gov/2024022961

British Library Cataloging-in-Publication Data available

Works by Lenard D. Moore

Poetry

Poems of Love and Understanding, Carlton Press, 1982
The Open Eye, North Carolina Haiku Society Press, 1985
Forever Home, St. Andrews College Press, 1992
Desert Storm: A Brief History, Los Hombres Press, 1993
A Temple Looming, WordTech Editions, 2008
The Geography of Jazz, Mountains and Rivers Press, 2018
Long Rain, Wet Cement Press, 2021
A Million Shadows at Noon, Cuttlefish Books, 2023

Anthologies or chapbooks (authored, edited, or coedited)

Gathering at the Crossroads: The Million Man March, Red Moon Press, 2003
Wild Again: Selected Haiku of Nina Wicker, coedited with Dave Russo and Jim Kacian, Red Moon Press, 2005
Beneath the Willow Tree: Poems from the North Carolina Haiku Society, Rosenberry Books, 2007
Dandelion Wind: 2007 Haiku North America Anthology, coedited with Michael Dylan Welch, Press Here, 2008
In the Night Shallows: Selected Haiku of Rebecca Ball Rust, coedited with Dave Russo, Rosenberry Books, 2009
The Stone House: An Anthology of Haiku from Bolin Brooks Farm, coedited with Dave Russo, Rosenberry Books, 2012
Learning to See the Truth, coedited with Dave Russo, Rosenberry Books, 2014
One Window's Light: A Collection of Haiku, Unicorn Press, 2017
All the Songs We Sing: Celebrating the 25th Anniversary of the Carolina African American Writers' Collective, Blair, 2020

Contents

Introduction   ix

Chronology   xvii

Innerview with Lenard D. Moore   3
   Jane Reichhold / 1995

The Open Eye of Lenard D. Moore: An Interview   9
   Doris Lucas Laryea / 1996

On Being and Becoming a Writer: Interview with Lenard D. Moore   26
   L. Teresa Church / 2009

A Haiku Consciousness: An Interview with Lenard D. Moore   41
   Sheila Smith McKoy / 2011

An Interview with Lenard D. Moore   46
   John Zheng / 2017

Mentoring a New Generation of African American Haiku Writers: Interview with Lenard D. Moore   60
   Crystal Simone Smith / 2020

Lenard D. Moore: An Interview   72
   David G. Lanoue / 2021

Lenard D. Moore on the Music of Poetry   77
   Ann Angel / 2021

Lenard Moore: Poet, Editor, Teacher, and Mentor   86
  Dee Clere / 2021

An Interview with Lenard D. Moore   94
  Toru Kiuchi / 2022

Interview with Lenard D. Moore   104
  Susan Antolin / 2022

Interview with Lenard D. Moore   111
  Sharon Hayes-Brown / 2022

Building Poems Like a Carpenter: Interview with Lenard D. Moore   127
  Lauri Scheyer / 2022

Jazz Poetry as a Message of African American Culture: An Interview with Lenard D. Moore   141
  John Zheng / 2023

Between Grief and the Gospel: The Poetry of Lenard D. Moore   152
  Ce Rosenow / 2023

Long Rain: An Interview with Lenard D. Moore   163
  Olga Ponomareva / 2023

Index   171

Introduction

Lenard D. Moore is a contemporary African American writer who has published eight poetry collections. He also served as the President of the Haiku Society of America from 2008 to 2009. Known internationally as a poet writing in the Japanese style, Moore has distinguished himself especially in such forms as jazz poetry, haiku, tanka, renga, sequence, and haibun, which present moments of aesthetic delights as well as a voice enriched with African American culture.

Moore's early writing shows his development as a haiku poet. It follows the expressive trend of traditional Japanese haiku and offers the reader a sensible experience, as shown in:

> Old deserted farm;
> spring whirlwind twirls peach petals
> over sunlit hills

This haiku adopts the five-seven-five pattern—the use of which has been discouraged in today's English haiku world—to show Moore's initial practice in haiku writing. The main image is the whirlwind, which seems destructive not only to the abandoned farm but also to the blooming peach petals twirled "over sunlit hills." Even the recurrences of alliteration, consonance, and assonance in the line of "spring whirlwind twirls peach petals" offers a moment to experience irresistible sounds of nature: *s*, *in*, *irl*, and *p*, showing Moore's interest in using sounds to create an auditory effect of nature on the ear.

Although the traditional three-line pattern of seventeen syllables has been helpful in his early haiku practice, Moore also seeks patterns with fewer syllable counts in each line, a trend in contemporary haiku writing to use less to convey more and to reveal true terseness essential to Japanese haiku. In "Shape of Things to Come," published in the autumn 2012 issue of *Modern Haiku*, Jim Kacian discussed this haiku trend:

> Haiku has evolved beyond its early stages into something leaner, stronger, sharper. It requires a better poet to write good haiku today, and more often what a poet chooses to write is less likely to be normative. Or put another way, what was normative to the best poets of previous generations is no longer competitive for the best poets of the current generation. . . . Increasingly we find more different kinds of haiku in these places, and readers are learning to parse them in new ways, just as poets are learning to exploit the new possibilities inherent in the new shapes. (23)

Kacian's argument is apt as each generation must have its own form. Doubtless, a good haiku poet will feel constrained by the five-seven-five pattern while developing his or her writing skills, and this feeling will urge him or her to seek a breakthrough by finding other forms of expression. Yet, this does not say that the normative haiku of previous generations must be judged or questioned by the standards of the current generation but that the current generation's form renovation will be a creative addition to contemporary American haiku.

It is evident that new forms of haiku do maintain the essence of terseness. They also resuscitate the English language and sophisticate the ways of creative expression. As an assiduous practitioner in the haiku mainstream, Moore has challenged himself to use fewer syllables. For instance,

> upturned cicada
> we read slave narratives
> row by row

The syllabic counts of this haiku are five, six, three, showing a free-verse style of haiku writing. Moore uses the upturned cicada image for an internal comparison with the reading of slave narratives. The "row by row" may have a double meaning to show an empathetic pain, making the reader to imagine that paragraphs become field rows where slaves labored. The juxtaposition through what is seen, read, and imagined reflects the poet's mindfulness of African American culture and history.

Moreover, Moore's economical use of words has pushed him to make his haiku even "leaner, stronger, sharper" with enhanced quality. Read this haiku—

> wind chimes:
> a robin stops
> to listen

—which demonstrates an effective progress of his haiku practice from following the normative five-seven-five pattern to using a freer two-four-three pattern. Its minimal form shows his adaptability to maintain the quality of fine haiku. The wind chimes ring for a reader to apprehend, associate, and appreciate the meaning beyond the words or behind the images: an invisible perceiver, who enjoys listening to the wind chimes, sees that even a robin nearby stops singing when drawn to the melodious sound. The use of images for the effect of synesthesia invites the reader's reaction to visual and auditory senses and the involvement of intellectual comprehension. The smooth assonance in "wind," "robin," and "listen" enriches the melody of this haiku as well.

In fact, understanding a new shape of haiku is necessary for the understanding of the poet's creative mind and the metaphysical linkage he creates. Moore is current in following the trend. His use of fewer words for more in meaning and aesthetic shows a phase in advancing his haiku writing, especially when a poetic form, which is originally foreign, works to enrich the mind and experience through language awareness and imagery function and to establish an aesthetic attitude toward the understanding of our age, our cultures, and our world. In other words, Moore's haiku practice is a process of gaining the marrow of haiku and its complexities, and this process challenges him to write with distinguishable freshness for the current generation.

Additionally, Moore's experiment with new shapes has led him to explore the one-line pattern, termed by Kacian as monoku, which resembles Japanese haiku in the true essence of terseness. Here's an example:

> eyes of a cat the fog

The cat and fog images immediately remind us of Carl Sandburg's imagistic poem "Fog." Both poems share the similarity in comparing fog to a cat. Sandburg's catlike fog is kinetic through a series of movements, and it is gigantic enough to engulf the harbor and the city, but Moore's haiku focuses on the cat's eyes, the ones of the silent, large cat-fog. Yet, the difference is that Sandburg's poem calls for obvious associative thinking of the two images, but Moore's resists such association because the relationship between the two images is deliberately ambiguous, showing a comparative instability that either way seems acceptable. The fog and the cat's eyes seem more objective than metaphorical, both presenting a sense of simplification of the two images. However, since a haiku consists of two interacting parts, the physical eyes of a cat can be a synecdoche to challenge the reader to juxtapose for an imaginative association. Then, we may ask: What does the synecdoche signify? The animality of the fog? The world with deception? Or a simple objective presentation of nature? These questions will help us dwell upon the dynamic relationship between the cat's eyes and the fog through associative thinking. Moore might have written this haiku with Sandburg's "Fog" in mind, but he surely added new wine to the old bottle with his own expression.

Moore is also a poet mindful of African American tradition and music, although many of his haiku show him as a nature poet. Here's a blues tanka from his recently published collection *Long Rain*:

> morning goes:
> the blues woman chants
> in the summer heat,
> while hanging the wash
> this end of the clothesline

Here the senses play for a synesthetic effect: the woman's blues chanting and laundry hanging in the summer heat, all of which invite us to not just hear but see and feel as well. The vivid presentation of the blues woman reminds us of Eudora Welty's photograph of a Black washerwoman in *One Time, One Place: Mississippi in the Depression*. It is evident that the Black washerwoman has been a favorite image for African American writers. For instance, Richard Wright, whose haiku has influenced Moore's early work, composed two haiku about Black washwomen. In haiku number 60, the glinting sun on "a washerwoman's black arms" in a cold creek does not provide soothing warmth but accentuates Blackness to indicate the suffering of a washerwoman. Like Wright, Moore is devoted to presenting African American experience through haiku.

As mentioned earlier in this introduction, Moore is best known as a haiku poet. His popularity in haiku seems to overshadow his talent in free verse. In fact, he has published two well-crafted poetry collections, *The Geography of Jazz* and *A Tempe of Looming*. Let's read "Lovebeat," a beautiful lyric poem about the oneness of love and music:

> My eyes close like blinds
> I pull shut in her bedroom
> as she draws me close enough

to stroke my lips.
"Take me," she nods
as if pulling notes
from Miles's horn.
Coltrane's music is gentle,
rain quenching jazzbuds open.

Love with a person and love with music interplay for a visual sensation of touch and feel. "Eyes close like blinds" indicates a private moment, and love in a trance is like "pulling notes / from Miles's horn" as well as Coltrane's gentle music, which becomes "rain quenching jazzbuds open"—the image of love that is physical, spiritual, and musical.

Included in *Conversations with Lenard D. Moore* are sixteen interviews, most of which were conducted in recent years as Moore has gained more spotlight in the haiku world. Although Moore writes different types of poetry, most of the interviews focus on his work in the Japanese genre, which has been an inseparable part of his creative life. To him, haiku does not stand alone as a foreign genre he has been in love with but a useful means that helps with his "longer forms of poetry," as admitted in his interview with Jane Reichhold: "I write haiku, tanka, and renga because it is a way of life, which is a part of me just as I have become a part of it. I find that haiku helps me to sharpen the focus of my longer forms of poetry. It helps with the precision of language and the contrast of images as they are able to establish the mood of the poem."

In the introduction of her interview, Doris Lucas Laryea praised Moore as "a poet whose strong, direct, and evocative poems connect generations, cross continents, and touch people everywhere, yet they are rooted in his African American culture." This root can be traced in Moore's jazz poetry found especially in *The Geography of Jazz*, which presents his jazz experience and feeling. To Moore, jazz is a celebration of African American culture as well as American culture. His fascination with music makes his poems rhythmic. He said about the influence of jazz in the interview with John Zheng: "I think breaths, rhythm, and feeling enable me to transcribe my voice into lines. The freedom of improvisation also enables me to transcribe my voice into lines when I write a jazz poem. Ancestral memory also enables me to transcribe my voice into lines. Without my ancestors, I would not have been able to do such work."

Another characteristic of African American culture reflected in Moore's poetry is the jazzku (jazz haiku), bluesku (blues haiku), and gospelku (gospel haiku), which can be considered collectively as variants of an African American haiku form to show Moore's approach to find a new way to present African American experience. Moore has said, "Yes, I am trying to create an African American haiku form. I have written jazz haiku and blues haiku which I have labeled or named jazzku and blueshu respectively" (Laryea). This form also shows that Moore's poetry is imbued with music, as he told Lauri Scheyer: "Music is certainly prominent in many of my poems. I started listening to music very early in my life. In fact, I listened to the choirs at my hometown church. When I was a teenager, I visited other churches and enjoyed listening to gospel songs. I also listened to R&B music early in life." It is evident, as a few interviews reveal, that Moore has not only incorporated music into his poetry but also performed his poetry with jazz musicians and jazz bands.

Music keeps flowing with Moore's creative work. In 2021, Moore published *Long Rain*, a collection of tanka. When asked about his idea of writing tanka, Moore said that his tanka should "resonate and sing." That is, it must have music in it. Tanka is another Japanese poetic form that has fascinated Moore for decades. In answering Olga Ponomareva's question about how Japanese culture and literature have taken root in his poetry, Moore explained, "I have appreciated Japanese culture and literature for decades. With my writing of poetry in Japanese poetic forms, I strive for cross-cultural reporting." In this sense, Moore is a Japanese poet living in North Carolina, as phrased by Guy Davenport in his introduction to *Long Rain*.

The interviews in *Conversations with Lenard D. Moore* are arranged chronologically according to the dates they were published or conducted. In short, the interviews offer us a clue about how a poet has developed his writing skills, how he has used these skills to present his cultural pride, and how music and tradition have been an inseparable part of his daily and creative life. As an African American poet, Moore believes that he is a spokesperson for his community. As the founder of the Carolina African American Writers' Collective, he has edited anthologies for its members because he realizes that African American writers need a platform to discuss their work for publication. He has also reached out to the community to teach, read, and perform poetry with a belief that a poet should be "a messenger for the people" (Laryea).

Conversations with Lenard D. Moore will not materialize without permissions to print or reprint these interviews. Therefore, I thank each interviewer and publisher sincerely for their support; I also thank Lenard D.

Moore wholeheartedly for his support and patience. Last, I express my deep gratitude to my editor, Mary Heath—an angel to work with over the years of editing several conversations books—series editor Monika Gehlawat, and all University Press of Mississippi staff for their staunch support of the publication of this book.

JZ

Chronology

1958	Born Lenard Duane Moore on February 13, in Jacksonville, North Carolina, to parents Rogers E. Moore and Mary L. Pearson.
1976	Graduates from White Oak High School in North Carolina.
1976	Attends Coastal Carolina Community College.
1978	Basic Training at Fort Jackson, South Carolina.
1978	Stationed at Fort Eustis, Virginia (1978–80).
1980	Deploys to Duty Station in Stuttgart, Germany.
1981	Honorable Discharge from US Army with the Good Conduct Medal.
1982	Publishes *Poems of Love and Understanding* (Carlton).
1983	Travels to San Diego and serves as the poet-in-residence at Mira Mesa Branch Library; accepted for California Poets in the Schools program; wins the Haiku Museum of Tokyo Award.
1984	Returns to Jacksonville, North Carolina; leaves for Raleigh and begins a job at Yakin Country Club and at North Carolina Department of Public Instruction or North Carolina Department of Education.
1985	Publishes *The Open Eye* (North Carolina Haiku Society Press).
1986	Publishes poems in *The Haiku Anthology*, edited by Cor Van Den Heuvel (Simon & Schuster).
1987	Contributing editor, *The Small Press Book Review* (1987–93); writer-in-residence, Wake County Arts Council, United Arts Council of Raleigh and Wake County (1987–94).
1988	Publishes *Poems for Performance*; associate editor for *Pine Needles* (North Carolina Haiku Society newsletter, 1988–90); staff reviewer, *Library Journal* (1988–95).
1990	Literary consultant and presenter, Humanities Extension Program, North Carolina State University (1990–95).
1992	Publishes *Forever Home* (St. Andrews); cofounder of the Washington Street Writers Group with Bruce Lader.
1993	Publishes *Desert Storm: A Brief History* (Los Hombres); begins

	undergraduate classes in CAPE Program at Shaw University; coeditor in chief of *Shawensis Magazine* (literary journal).
1994	Wins the Haiku Museum of Tokyo Award.
1995	Graduates from Shaw University with a BA in liberal studies with a minor in English (magna cum laude); elected as executive chairman of the North Carolina Haiku Society; leaves the North Carolina Department of Public Instruction; teaches high school English at Enloe Magnet High School, North Carolina; founds the Carolina African American Writers' Collective; executive chairman of the North Carolina Haiku Society (1995–97).
1996	Attends graduate school and serves as an editorial assistant for *All That Jazz*, English Department, North Carolina A&T State University; publishes second printing of *Forever Home*; receives the Indies Arts Award.
1997	Graduates from NC A&T State University with MA in English and African American literature; wins the College Language Association Margaret Walker Award; begins as visiting lecturer, English Department, at North Carolina State University; literary consultant and presenter, Humanities Extension Program, North Carolina State University (1997–2001).
1998	Begins as adjunct English instructor in the CAPE Program at Shaw University; receives the Tar Heel of the Week Award; receives Cave Canem Fellowship; longtime executive chairman of the North Carolina Haiku Society (1998–present).
1999	Receives Cave Canem Fellowship.
2000	Visiting lecturer at North Carolina State University; receives Cave Canem Fellowship; serves as a guest editor for *Drumvoices Revue: A Confluence of Literary, Cultural & Vision Arts*.
2002	Serves as a writer-counselor at the National Book Foundation Summer Writing Camp.
2003	Wins the Haiku Museum of Tokyo Award; publishes *Gathering at the Crossroad: The Million Man March* with photography by Eugene B. Redmond (Red Moon); serves as a Writer-Counselor at the National Book Foundation Summer Writing Camp (2003–5).
2005	Accepts temporary position as instructor of English at Mount Olive College; coedits *Wild Again: Selected Haiku of Nina Wicker* with Dave Russo and Jim Kacian (Red Moon).
2006	Hired as full-time faculty and promoted to assistant professor of English; faculty advisor for *The Olive Branch* (later became *Trojan*

	Voices) literary journal (2006–14); receives the Sam Ragan Award in the Fine Arts.
2007	Organizes with Bob Moyer and Dave Russo the 2007 Haiku North America Conference in Winston-Salem, North Carolina; edits and publishes the anthology *Beneath the Willow Tree: Poems from the North Carolina Haiku Society* (Rosenberry Books); receives Soul Mountain Retreat Fellowship; publishes poem "Black Girl Tap Dancing" in the textbook *Poetry: An Introduction*, edited by Michael Meyer (Bedford/St. Martin's).
2008	Publishes *A Temple Looming* (WordTech Editions); coedits with Michael Dylan Welch *Dandelion Wind: An Anthology of Poems* commemorating the 2007 Haiku North America conference; receives the Raleigh Medal of the Arts for Lifetime Achievement in the Arts; elected first African American president of the Haiku Society of America.
2009	Coedits with Dave Russo *In The Night Shallows: Selected Haiku of Rebecca Ball Rust* (Rosenberry Books); elected again for another term as president of the Haiku Society of America; invited to International Symposium on Haiku for the Haiku International Association 20th Anniversary, in Tokyo, Japan.
2010	Guest edits "Aforebo: A Harvest of North Carolina Writers of African Descent" with "A Tribute to Carolina African American Writers' Collective" for *Obsidian: Literature in the African Diaspora*.
2011	Guest edits *Solo Café 8&9: Teachers & Students* (Solo).
2012	Publishes *The Stone House: An Anthology of Haiku from Bolin Brook Farm*, coedited with Dave Russo (Rosenberry Books).
2013	Publishes the anthology *7*, coedited with Roberta Beary (Jacar); publishes poems in *Haiku in English: The First Hundred Years* (Norton); edits *Solo Café 8&9: Teachers & Students*, volume 2 (Solo).
2014	Receives the North Carolina Award for Literature; reads and performs poetry accompanied by saxophonist James Dallas on BLACK NOUVEAU, Program #226, Milwaukee Public Television; coedits with Dave Russo *Learning to See the Truth* (Rosenberry Books); receives Furious Flower Laureate Ring at the Laureate's Luncheon at 2014 Furious Flower Poetry Conference.
2015	Publishes thirtieth-anniversary edition of *The Open Eye* (Mountains and Rivers).

2017   Publishes *One Window's Light: A Collection of Haiku* (Unicorn),

2018   Publishes *The Geography of Jazz* (Mountains and Rivers); awarded the 2018 Haiku Society of America Mildred Kanterman Merit Book Award for *One Window's Light: A Collection of Haiku* for the best anthology published in 2017; serves as a judge for the statewide Poetry Out Loud competition; poetry performance with the University of Mount Olive Jazz Band at Wayne County Arts Council in Goldsboro.

2019   Reads and performs poetry accompanied by Bassist Alrick Huebener at VerseFest 2019 in Ottawa, Canada; honoree of the 2019 Black History Month in the governor's mansion.

2020   Publishes *All the Songs We Sing: Celebrating the 25th Anniversary of the Carolina African American Writers' Collective* (Blair); publishes new edition of *The Geography of Jazz* (Blair); appointed Honorary Curator of the American Haiku Archives at California State Library in Sacramento (2020–21).

2021   Reads as a featured poet on *The Poet and the Poem*; interviews by Grace Cavalieri; and publishes *Long Rain* (Wet Cement).

2022   North Carolina Poetry Society *Pinesong* anthology dedicatee.

2023   Publishes *A Million Shadows at Noon* (Cuttlefish Books).

Conversations with
Lenard D. Moore

Innerview with Lenard D. Moore

Jane Reichhold / 1995

From *Mirrors* (Winter 1995). Reprinted by permission of Lenard D. Moore.

Jane Reichhold: Lenard, the more I know you, the more astounded I am by all you do and the many kinds of literature in which you are involved. Perhaps it is best to start with finding out what you have done.

Lenard D. Moore: First of all, let me say that I think it's interesting that you call this an innerview. It seems as if you are trying to communicate with the poet's inner spirit-mind. I have been writing haiku and tanka for over twelve years. My first renga was written with Mary Smith and Barbara McCoy eleven years ago. I have also written other forms of Oriental poetry for more than a decade. I have had haiku and tanka published in over thirty literary journals as well as in the traditional haiku magazines.

I especially like writing narrative poems and dramatic monologues. I have completed a half dozen short stories, and I have a novel about one-third completed. My book reviews and essays have appeared in numerous publications. For six years I served as writer-in-residence for the United Arts Council of Raleigh and Wake County; two years as associate editor of *Pine Needles* (the newsletter of the North Carolina Haiku Society); seven years as contributing editor of *The Small Press Book Review*; four years as a literacy consultant for North Carolina State University's Humanities Extension OUTREACH program; six years as staff reviewer for *Library Journal*; one year as regional director of the International Black Writers Conference, Inc; one year as acting advisor to *Pacific Moana Quarterly* (New Zealand); one year as a magazine consultant for the *Black Writer* magazine; two years as coeditor in chief of *Shawensis Magazine* (the Shaw University literary magazine); two years on the North Carolina Writers' Network's board of directors; four years on North Carolina Writers' Network's Black Writers' Identification Program Committee; one year on the North Carolina Writers' Network's Fall Conference Committee; eleven years on the Executive

Committee of the North Carolina Haiku Society. I have served on the Work Performance Management Review Task Force, Employee Appreciation Week Committee, Grievance Committee, and (currently) the Quality Council at the North Carolina Department of Public Instruction. I have served on the Kuumba Festival Committee; Artist Housing Task Force (City of Raleigh Arts Commission); Individual Artists' Support Task Force (United Arts Council of Raleigh and Wake County, Inc.), among other committees for various organizations. I have judged numerous poetry contests for local, regional, and national writers/poetry groups and/or organizations. I am the founder of the Carolina African American Writers' Collective. Ten years ago, I was awarded the CTM (Competent Toastmaster) award by Toastmasters International. I won the Jacksonville (North Carolina) Toastmasters Club's public speaking competition, then placed third in the district competition the same year.

JR: On what are you currently focusing?

LDM: I am currently focusing on writing more poems about the effects of the Vietnam War from a son's perspective of a Vietnam veteran. My father served two tours of duty in Vietnam. I talk to him from time to time about certain events that happened in that particular war. So, I am finishing this collection of Vietnam poems that I started a few years ago. I am also writing more jazz poems and blues poems to complete a collection of them that I started eight years ago. Those poems come to me by listening to jazz and blues. Some of those poems come to me by impression or by what my eyes actually see at a jazz festival or a blues festival. I first wrote the story "The Little People" when I was in the tenth grade. I still have one or two other short stories that I wrote in the tenth grade, which I plan to take another look at and rewrite for a possible children's book. I have a rather long haiku sequence that I wrote two years ago, which I may turn into a children's book.

JR: How did you begin to write haiku?

LDM: It was in January of 1982. I was in bed sick with the flu. I happened to notice my literature textbook on the dresser and started reading the poems. It was a book that I had as a textbook in a class I took at the University of Maryland. I saw a translation of a Japanese haiku master in the book. So, I thought I would try to write some haiku. But they were not good haiku. Then I attended the Annual North Carolina Poetry Festival at the Weymouth Center in Southern Pines in June of 1982. There I met an old man named Hale Kellog who talked to me about haiku and the purity of it. He read me several of his first haiku that were published in *Modern Haiku*.

Dragonfly was one of the first magazines that published my haiku, and its editor, Lorraine Ellis Harr, was very helpful in offering comments on haiku submissions. I also read everything that I could find about haiku, including Harold G. Henderson's classic *Introduction to Haiku*. Yet I wrote haiku as often as possible to help with my craft.

JR: Why do you continue to write haiku, tanka, and renga when you are so adept in prose and other poetry?

LDM: I write haiku, tanka, and renga because it is a way of life, which is a part of me just as I have become a part of it. I find that haiku helps me to sharpen the focus of my longer forms of poetry. It helps with the precision of language and the contrast of images as they are able to establish the mood of the poem. I find that tanka helps me to stretch the haiku moment or expand what might have been a haiku for me. I can deal with relationships more fully in a tanka than in a haiku. I can also create a poem that is more lyrical when writing tanka than when writing a haiku. I find renga to be very challenging and demanding when I am working in that particular form. Renga takes me in directions I wouldn't have otherwise taken. And that is fun for me, especially when writing a renga with an individual or individuals who fall into harmony with whatever the theme might be. I like the turns that renga takes as it progresses from link to link. I find that tanka helps with my haiku writing as I filter through whatever natural phenomena that I might encounter to inform my haiku.

JR: What percentage of your total literary work time is devoted to the Japanese genre?

LDM: I would say 25 percent of my total literary work is devoted to the Japanese genre. Yet, there are times when I work only in the Japanese genre. For example, last month (October 1994) I was completing my book-length manuscript of tanka, *A Point of Light*.

JR: We all write from where we are. You have a special place in the haiku community because you are one of the only two or three African Americans. Do you consciously let this fact play a role in your writing?

LDM: I totally agree with you. Certainly, I write from where I am. I feel totally connected to my homeplace. It is something that can easily be detected in much of my haiku as well as in my other literary works. I have written a considerable number of haiku about my garden. I have also written about the various places I have lived, including San Diego and Germany.

I am aware that I am one of a very few African Americans writing haiku as you have mentioned, but I don't think I consciously let that fact play a major role in my haiku writing. Yet, there are a great number of my haiku that allude to the fact of who I am. I say this because I must write from my own experiences.

JR: As a Euro-American, I feel I cannot write Japanese-style haiku, but to be honest, I must marry the Japanese genre to my literary and cultural background. Is this process different for you, or does the fact you and I are both Americans writing in English mean we are working from the same well of experiences?

LDM: I, too, feel I cannot write Japanese-style haiku. Yes, that's exactly right. As you have realized, I use my cultural and literary background to write the Japanese genre. For that reason, I hope I am bringing something new. There are certain things, however, that make a haiku what it is, including form. But I write about or incorporate blues, jazz, and other things that are directly related to the African American community. So, in that sense, the process would be different for you and me because our experiences are so different. Of course, there are such differences as food, clothing, language, music, and so forth. So, things wouldn't be quite the same, though we are both Americans creating or writing our haiku in English.

JR: Would you care to comment on Alice Walker's book of haiku, *Once*?

LDM: I have not seen the book. I have read the haiku of Richard Wright, Sonia Sanchez, and Etheridge Knight. It is evident that their haiku were written from their own experiences. Francis W. Alexander is an African American who has been writing and publishing in the haiku community for a few years. Sharon Agnew is an African American who has recently started working in the haiku community. There are a few other African Americans who write and publish haiku from time to time, such as Kalamu ya Salaam.

JR: Would you open the door to your study so *Mirrors* readers may see where you work?

LDM: My study is downstairs in the family room. I call it my personal library. Shelves of books and magazines line the walls. Piles of books and magazines are on a table that my mother and father gave us. I am referring to my wife, Lynn, and daughter, Maiisha, who have both written and published haiku poetry. There is studio-like stereo equipment along the far-right wall. Numerous audio cassettes of music, well-known poets reading their poetry, and interviews of me on radio shows are on the stereo shelves, along with poetry posters and broadsides. Hundreds of record albums or LPs are in black plastic album cases. Stacks of VHS videocassettes of my poetry readings, interviews on talk shows, educational programs, cultural programs, movies, family gatherings, and sports are on top of books in a corner. A Japanese vase, well over a hundred years old, and two African ceramic heads sit on the fireplace mantel. A dark blue sofa sits in front of the long floor-model TV. A dark-blue loveseat sits adjacent to the sofa. A VCR rests on top of the TV, though the cable is hooked into the TV for cable channels. There are trophies that our daughter won for a talent show, and track and field, shining on top of the TV. Her trophies stand beside the trophies that I won for basketball over the years. A long, waist-high, wall-length shelf is built on the left wall as you enter the family room. Paneling covers the walls all around the room. Light-blue carpet covers the floor. Mugs and other artifacts that I collected in Germany are on shelves. Dried flowers are arranged in vases beside the stereo components on shellacked shelves. A chandelier hangs from the plastered ceiling. I also write on the second floor at the dining room table, too, where I do my typing. I also write on the third floor in the bedroom. And in addition, I write at my mother and father's house whenever I go to visit them. I have written a number of my works at public libraries and college libraries around the country.

JR: *Desert Storm* is your most recent book of haiku. Where can one obtain a copy?

LDM: Yes, *Desert Storm: A Brief History* is my most recently published book. I would like to comment on that particular book if I may do so. My brother, Jerome, served in Desert Storm in an artillery unit. Before he left for Desert Storm, I had a dream one night in which he told me he was going to Saudi Arabia. Two weeks later, I received a phone call when he actually told me he was going there. When my brother returned, he told me that wild dogs were eating dead soldiers, among other things that happened over there. This is just to point out that nothing in my book, *Desert Storm: A Brief History*, came from TV. I realize that what is seen on TV is reported from a biased opinion. I also have served three years in the United States Army on active duty. So, I feel that I knew enough about what was going on to write that book. I saw photographs of Desert Storm's aftermath, which were quite graphic not to mention the other Desert Storm veterans that I talked to. Yet, I am most pleased with how well my book has been received by Vietnam veterans and Desert Storm veterans alike. It received a rave review in *Vietnam Generation*, among several other publications. I have given poetry readings in military towns, and *Desert Storm: A Brief History* has sold well. Those poetry readings were filled to capacity. The military personnel usually begin telling me their experiences and war stories. The book was published by Los Hombres Press, which is in San Diego. However, the book is already out of print. But several copies are available at the Know Bookstore in Charlotte, North Carolina. Bruce Bridges is the owner. I do have a book of longer poems, *Forever Home*, which is currently available from St. Andrew's College Press.

It is important for individuals who might be interested in reviewing my literary career to consider my first book of haiku, *The Open Eye*. This book was published by the North Carolina Haiku Society Press. It appeared in print in 1985, but it's no longer available. The haiku in that book are seasonally arranged and depict the southern landscape where I grew up.

JR: What do your readers have to look forward to in your next book?

LDM: I can only say that I have been working on a number of haiku about various subjects. I have enough haiku to do a book of garden haiku, a book of telephone haiku, and a book of travel haiku. I also have enough haiku about various other subjects such as jazz, blues, sports, and working, among other things. I like the fact that I have so many options open to me. So, I will go from there. Let's see what happens.

The Open Eye of Lenard D. Moore: An Interview

Doris Lucas Laryea / 1996

From *Obsidian II* 11, no. 1/2 (1996): 159–84. Reprinted by permission of Lenard D. Moore.

Lenard Duane Moore is a poet whose strong, direct, and evocative poems connect generations, cross continents, and touch people everywhere, yet they are rooted in his African American culture. Moore is at the forefront of a new African American literary renaissance of the nineteen nineties, and as we move toward the twenty-first century, he is helping to create and shape a new African American literary canon. His poems are extensions of himself—uncluttered, full of compassion and wonder for people and for nature. One of the most striking aspects of Moore's work is his poignancy in using a variety of poetic forms. He is as comfortable in writing traditional Western lyrical poetry as he is in mastering Eastern or Japanese poetic forms.

Doris Lucas Laryea: Why do you write?
Lenard D. Moore: I write because it is my way of life. I must write to survive. Writing is like a beating heart, a vital organ that keeps history and heritage alive. Writing is as crucial as inhaling and exhaling. In addition, I write to learn, to stay in touch with my inner self, to make sense of the past, present, and future, to inform and entertain, and to celebrate our existence.
Laryea: What started you writing?
Moore: Well, I usually tell people that I started writing in the army. You know how that goes. Of course, I wrote letters home to my girlfriend. I felt that I had to take special attention to those letters to keep her thinking about me while I was away. So, I tried to write poetic letters. Then I began writing poems and would include a poem or two with my letters. Those poems must have grabbed her in some way because she's my wife.

Laryea: Was there anything in your early life that gave you an intense desire to want to write about it?

Moore: I really enjoyed reading books in elementary school. My love for books early on did in fact contribute to my becoming a writer. I loved words and the way they worked together. Yeah, it must have been the words themselves. I remember being surrounded by books because my mother and father had books throughout the house. My father often would share the cost with me whenever I wanted to buy a set of books. I have a close-knit family made up of my parents, two sisters, and four brothers who have all helped me really to know how people think and feel about certain things. When I was growing up, my siblings and I were very active in sports and in the church. This has been valuable to my work. Let me also mention my grandfather. When I was very young, my grandfather, Luther T. Pearson, would tell us lots of stories. We enjoyed hearing them. I know I especially did. The manner by which he told his stories fascinated me. I've never forgotten his stories, and from time to time I find his presence in my poetry. In fact, he is the subject of "Why Grandpa Speaks with Dignity," a poem I like very much, and "On Summer Days," [an award-winning poem].

Laryea: I especially like in "Telling of Tales," when you write that your "Grandfather's dark eyes / lock on our young souls. / Honeysuckle sway, / scent the air. / Watery eyes stare back, we sit still." What is poetry?

Moore: Poetry is the language that touches our innermost feelings, language that is at once lyrical, imagistic, magical, and mystical, and language that is concisely written; it is innovative to the core and imbues readers and listeners with the history of the ever-changing times. Poetry is the touchstone of our human existence; it lets us be. . . . Poetry is everything that makes the earth, and the earth itself is a poem rotating toward infinity. Open, look, listen, and write.

Laryea: In reading your work, I've noticed that your poetry, like Gwendolyn Brooks's poetry, bridges generations and touches people around the world. It spans races and cultures, yet it is grounded and anchored in the African American experience.

Moore: Thank you for the insightful comment about my poetry. I am really glad that you see a connection in my poetry with Gwendolyn Brooks because I admire her poetry so much. I am certainly very much concerned with being able to evoke emotions within people around the world.

Laryea: What is an African American poet, and what do you think ought to be his or her purpose as a creative artist?

Moore: An African American poet is first an African American who happens to be a poet. The African American poet is a spokesperson for his or her community. The goals and functions of the African American poet are to inform his or her readers and to be a messenger for the people. He or she must function as that pipeline from community to all other lands throughout the world. The purpose of an African American poet is to educate and bring about social change for the people of the world to live in harmony with one another and the natural world. Hopefully, a sense of equality will derive from all of this. An African American poet certainly has to record and report a precise history for future generations. All of this must be accomplished with the most musical and powerful language possible. As an African American poet, I seek to write the best poem that God allows to flow from my blood, beat with my heart, and soar with my soul.

Laryea: What audience do you try to reach?

Moore: Certainly, I seek to please myself. Then I am able to please my audience. I feel that my primary audience is an African American one. I write for people who have an interest in poetry. When writing poetry, I try to use connections to transcend whatever experience or memory I want to replay for the reader. I just write the raw material down. Then I ponder over it to rework it into art. Usually, a poem takes unexpected twists and sometimes brings surprises. That's when I know the poem has communicated what I wanted it to. I especially aim to evoke some emotions deep within the reader. Somehow, I know when one of my poems just isn't right. It's just like when I grow vegetables in my garden. I can tell when a cucumber is frail or when a tomato isn't ripe. So, I think it's the same way with a poem. I have to nurture my poems to ensure that they will be an abundant harvest for my readers' ears and eyes. I want my poems to grab my readers by the doorknobs of their hearts and go inside without ever leaving, but I believe that my poetry is global. I hope that all races can appreciate the subjects that I write about and the way that I write about them.

Laryea: Your poetry is already appreciated by others. I understand that many of your works have been translated.

Moore: Yes. They have been translated into Spanish, Italian, Japanese, Croatian, Chinese, and Romanian. My poems appear in print on every continent.

Laryea: Let me congratulate you on having received this past April the College Language Association Creative Writing Award for Poetry (the Margaret Walker Award) for the poem "The Hat Maker, an Homage to My Mother." Would you talk about its evolution and what you were trying to do in it?

Moore: Thank you very much. My mother requested me to write a poem for her retirement celebration on November 2, 1996. My mother had been designing and making hats for several years. I would watch her and study how she arrived at certain designs. These observations became the kernel of the poem. It is a rather long poem with five sections—each with its own subtitle. "The Hat Maker, an Homage to My Mother" was originally the fifth section. I decided that this section could stand alone, complete within itself. I wanted to make sure the poem was "right" because my mother always made sure she used the "right" materials, angles, and so on in her hat creations. I felt that I owed her talent the same level of skill, so I tried to use the best diction, syntax, and texture that I felt accomplished this purpose. I am glad the poem has been well received because women who live all over the East Coast wear my mother's hats. The poem is among my favorites.

Laryea: Eudora Welty once said that "from the dawn of man's imagination, place has enshrined the spirit; as soon as man stopped wandering and stood still and looked about him, he found a god in that place; and from then on, that was where the god abided and spoke from if ever he spoke." Do you agree with her? How loyal to place are you?

Moore: Yes, I agree with Eudora Welty's statement. The sense of place is very important in my work because I feel a great kinship to the land of my hometown and its people and customs. I am interested in the geography and geology of Piney Green Community in Jacksonville, North Carolina. I am also very much interested in genealogy.

Laryea: Do you see yourself as a southern poet? Does this region of the United States serve as a distinguishing feature in your poems?

Moore: I am from the South, of the South, about the South, and live in the South. I feel that I am a southern poet in that sense, but I find many other subjects that may or may not belong to the South that enter my work. Still, the South has served as a motif in much of what I do. You may have noticed in *Forever Home* that the complexity of things enters my poetry, and the sense of place is important in the Japanese poetic forms that I use, too.

Laryea: I enjoyed reading *Forever Home*. Your close attention to detail, the openness of your eye, the richness and exactness of your language are still with me. I know the small old barn where "a horse stands munching hay, / waiting for water." I feel the hot rays of the sun as they fall "facedown / upon a wilted row / of rain dancing / mild windblown tobacco / plants," and I hear the "crickets on the airwaves" as "their shrills rise toward pinetops." They are mine. I am there. I am glad to hear that *Forever Home* has entered its second printing. It is a lovely book. I agree with Michel Fabre when he says the poems in *Forever Home* are "like still lives, landscapes, mottoes, and meditations." Is this your major collection?

Moore: Yes, *Forever Home* is my major collection of poetry, and much of it is autobiographical. I reflect upon my experiences in my hometown to weave into art that, hopefully, will strike some familiarity within my readers as my poems have done for you. Family, farm life, and the land are what I came to appreciate greatly in boyhood. I grew up in the rural South and did a lot of farm work. Such experiences enter my writing from time to time.

Laryea: The lead poem in *Forever Home* is "The Homeplace," and you write quite warmly about your ancestors whose "voices of former life / do not speak, their spirits huddling / into themselves, a brotherhood of saints." Would you comment on "The Homeplace?"

Moore: It's a free verse poem, which consists of four stanzas, rich in allegory and symbolism and rooted in geography and history. I enjoyed writing it. The speaker is acutely aware of the beauty of the landscape and of his ancestors' spirits and calls them "a brotherhood of saints." He wishes to grow old so that he can pass the experience to his next generation of kinfolk. There are sound and silence that interplay with symbolism. Further, motion supersedes time and space. The speaker mentions, "My eyes will not let go." In addition, memory won't let go either. But there is no doubt that the speaker has gotten meaning from "the homeplace" that he celebrates, and as a result, the speaker begins the next to last line of the poem with an inclusive "we," which informs the reader that the speaker feels that he has a message for the masses.

Laryea: Your first published book, entitled *The Open Eye*, appeared in 1985. I like the title and wonder if you would talk about it and about the structure of the work.

Moore: The meaning of the open eye is having the sharpest visual perceptions, being able to still the moment, and arousing emotions in the reader. I believe that all these things must be connected for the poet so that he or she has what I call the open eye. Thus, this is the reason I gave my first haiku collection the title *The Open Eye*. I was focusing on the miniature things in the natural world. I wrote the poems from an objective perspective. I was aiming to frame natural moments like a photographer. Structurally, the book is divided into four sections: "Spring," "Summer," "Autumn," and "Winter." The book unfolds like the phases of life—from birth to death. You know, it works like our very own existence. The haiku ranges from one to two per page. Anyway, there is a progression like aging throughout the book. Yet there is a oneness of human existence and the natural world in *The Open Eye*. I hope the book sheds some light on the lifeway.

Laryea: There are certainly some memorable haiku in *The Open Eye*. I've noticed that a few of them have been reprinted in *The Haiku Anthology*; *Haiku Moment: An Anthology of Contemporary North American Haiku*; and *Our Words, Our Ways: Reading and Writing in North Carolina*. I believe some of your more recent haiku appear in *Haiku World: An International Poetry Almanac*. One of my favorites in *The Open Eye* is the one about the old woman. Would you say a few words about this haiku?

Moore: The old woman haiku was awarded the Haiku Museum of Tokyo Award. It reads:

> the old woman
> looking into the stars
> sky all snowy

This haiku moves from the small being, the old woman, to the more expansive universe, the sky. The vowel sounds contribute to the pleasing rhythm of the poem. The alliteration of the *s* sounds enhances the music, too. The old woman has aged and is nearing death. So, there is darkness moving in on her life, but there is a great contrast of light within the stars. There is also a contrast of new birth or purity within the snow. There is irony as the old woman looks toward the heavens, possibly for a prayer. Instead, snow falls on her. The two *o*'s in "looking" give a visual effect of two eyes stars. So "looking" is the right word. The first and third lines have four syllables while the second line has six syllables. So, there is a great economy of words that strikes a responsive chord in the reader. In addition, this poem is full of details and renders a visual effect with "old woman," "stars," "sky," and "snowy." The reader knows what all four of these look like in his or her mind, yet there is beauty in the old woman's eyes staring into the stars as they stare back at her. There is an abundance of silence in this poem, too. The "ing" contributes to the continuous motion within the poem.

Laryea: Let's talk further about your use of Japanese poetic forms. You are recognized around the world as one of the few African American poets today who use Japanese forms, especially haiku, that highly compressed form of traditional poetry that is a formidable challenge for the poet. You are the only African American to win a number of outstanding haiku awards. You have won a Harold G. Henderson Award from the Haiku Society of America; twice you have won the Haiku Museum of Tokyo Award in

Japan, and you have served as the chairman of the North Carolina Haiku Society. What got you interested in this art form?

Moore: It was during the winter of 1982, January or February, when I was in bed with the flu that I noticed on my dresser an old literature book of mine, which I had used as a textbook in a college course at the University of Maryland Overseas Branch (Stuttgart, Germany). I started looking through the book and noticed some very short poems by Japanese poets translated into English. I read them and thought that I could write some of them myself. At first, I thought that they were just little simple poems. But I soon found out that wasn't the case. So, my first attempts were not successful at all. Later, in June of 1982, I attended the North Carolina Poetry Festival at Weymouth Center in Southern Pines, North Carolina. There I met an old man, Hale Kellog, who talked to me for about an hour or two, telling me about the purity of haiku and nature being the subject of haiku. He read me several of his haiku that were published in *Modern Haiku*. I was amazed at how much could be said in so few words. So, I began my crusade to record whatever I perceived in nature. Since then, I've tried to write haiku as often as possible. I have studied the form too. Dealing with the discipline of image and careful attention to language in haiku, I believe I have strengthened my writing of longer forms of poetry. I have maximized what I learned in haiku to write a book-length haiku sequence titled *Desert Storm: A Brief History*.

Laryea: I will come back to *Desert Storm* later. I am aware that not many African American poets write haiku regularly, and you do not adhere to any conventional haiku syllabic form. To what extent do you see yourself as a haiku poet working out of an African American aesthetic tradition?

Moore: I write haiku completely out of an African American aesthetic tradition. However, I do believe it took me a while to understand the haiku form and what I was doing before I reached the present stage in my writing. Certainly, there is an African American aesthetic tradition within haiku poetry. Richard Wright, Etheridge Knight, Sonia Sanchez, and Kalamu ya Salaam have written very notable haiku poetry. My haiku really deepened when I read Richard Wright's haiku about snow turning a boy's palms white as he was laughing and Etheridge Knight's haiku about convicts being compared to lizards and the tower glinting where the guard was keeping watch.

Laryea: So, there is a tradition that you must pay homage to.

Moore: Yes, but I was not aware of their haiku poetry until a few years after I had been writing haiku. What I want to do is write haiku that is rooted in the African American experience, but which speaks to all races.

Laryea: And how do you define African American aesthetics?

Moore: To me, African American aesthetics is an art that is eloquently Black through its rhythms, cultural allusions, historical references, and sociopolitical impact. African American aesthetics is constantly evolving, which ensures that African American art is always new. So, my own approach is always to create new poetry.

Laryea: Is that why you call your haiku "contemporary"? Are you trying to create an African American haiku form?

Moore: Yes, I am trying to create an African American haiku form. I have written jazz haiku and blues haiku which I have labeled or named jazzku and bluesku, respectively. I am always bending the rules of haiku poetry to make them my own, to capture the pulse of the African American community.

Laryea: Traditional Japanese haiku has three unrhymed lines of five, seven, and five syllables respectively, and usually it deals with some aspect of nature. You often shorten the number of syllables to four, eight, and five, and I've noticed you even use other syllabic indicators, even a one-line format. You write:

September warmth—
on watermelons the shadows
of migrant workers.

The poem gives a sharp, clear image, and it *suggests* more than what it actually *says*. It evokes within me contemplation and leaves me lingering in thought. I am there. I watch the migrant workers as they bend to pluck the melons from the brown, green, and yellow vines. Your language is uncluttered, and, like Walt Whitman, your eye sees the smallest creation of nature. The simplicity of the art form is what captures my interest.

Moore: Yes, I like to feel what I write, smell the cornbread cooking and the honeysuckle, hear the dogs barking and the cicadas singing, see the farmers.

Laryea: Do you do this in bluesku and jazzku?

Moore: Yes, bluesku and jazzku are uniquely Black in their allusions and music. They are short poems with expansive effects that inform who we are as a people.

Laryea: In "Jazzku," you write: "jazzwoman moaning / to the heart / riff I stir in / the almost midnight," and in "Bluesku 2" you write: "September sun flares / bald man rubs bass violin / into blooming blues." What do you hope to communicate to the reader in these forms?

Moore: In what I call bluesku, I try to evoke the pain and tone of the blues with a rhythm that is at once fluid and musical. I maintain the use of the kigo (season word) in the poems, but in my "blues tanka," I build upon what I do in bluesku by rhyming in the last two lines. Jazzku is an effort to evoke excitement and tone within jazz with allusions to both jazz songs and artists. I am careful about word choice to paint sharp contrasts in my jazzku, and the line breaks are not predictable. Jazzku works like jazz.

Laryea: What determines that an experience should be recorded as haiku and not as lyrical poetry?

Moore: I usually opt to write a haiku when I want to freeze some great moment in time. I mean a phenomenon that needs to be recorded. That's what compels me to write a haiku. Yet a successful haiku has a stark contrast of images in it. And the kigo that I use informs the reader which season the haiku takes place. Otherwise, I use another form to reach my readers.

Laryea: Is that why you chose the haiku form in *Desert Storm*—to freeze a moment in time?

Moore: I wanted to do something new within the African American literary canon by writing a long poem or sequence, using the haiku form. The book includes gender roles and race relations. For the most part, the events in the book are chronologically arranged. There is the issue of family relations in the book, too. Nonetheless, it is important to note that, unlike the Vietnam War, there is much community support among American civilians for American soldiers in *Desert Storm: A Brief History*.

Laryea: I find this book-length poem to be a study of history, biography, psychology, and sociology. *Desert Storm* is a unified work of art—a poetic moment in history that opens on "September sunrise / Marine leaving for the Persian Gulf / looks back at his wife" and ends with "back home / soldier listens to birdcalls / marking sunrise." The book is a succession of unforgettable images, but the image of war is supreme. You write: "a grenade explodes / shadows of soldiers skirting / the desert road"; and "bomb after bomb / smoking up the night desert / the cries of soldiers." Then there is "a Black soldier / breathing into a saxophone / hot desert wind" as one pictures "two sweaty GIs / stacking sandbags in a trench / far off bombs." One can see the "soldiers running / along the barb-wired border / moonless night." Since you did not experience the Persian Gulf War firsthand, what sort of research did you do for *Desert Storm: A Brief History*?

Moore: Of course, I talked to my brother Jerome, who fought in an artillery unit in the Gulf War or Desert Storm. He talked at length about how a Vietnam veteran buddy helped him to prepare for the war while they waited for the first guns to sound. I remember once about three o'clock in the morning, when I was home visiting my mother and father, the phone rang.

My mother ran to the other end of the house to my childhood room, and she told me to answer the phone, thinking that the phone call might bring bad news about my brother. I answered the phone, and my brother Jerome was on the other end of the line.

Yet what touched me the most was when my father, who was very ill, got on the phone and told my brother to make certain that he stays down in his foxhole, make certain that enough sandbags are in it, and keep his helmet on his head. I had never heard my father talk that way. But I was aware that he had served two duty tours in Vietnam.

Also, I served three years in the United States Army. So, I understood warfare and the training and how certain weapons work.

In addition, I viewed stacks of photographs that depicted the aftermath of Desert Storm. I saw a burned body still sitting behind the steering wheel of a bombed military truck, a human head blown into pieces on the desert sand, American soldiers standing over the deceased Iraqi soldiers, and so forth. The photographs were very graphic. When my brother returned from the Gulf, he talked very openly about how wild dogs were eating the dead soldiers. He talked about actual conflicts during the war, too. Then I talked to other Desert Storm veterans who willingly shared their experiences with me. So that is the sort of research that I did for my book, *Desert Storm: A Brief History*.

Laryea: Comment on other Japanese art forms you use.

Moore: Other than haiku, I write senryu, tanka, renga, and haiku sequences on a very regular basis. I have recently finished writing a book-length manuscript of tanka, which is tentatively titled *A Point of Light*.

Laryea: What is it like?

Moore: It is a collection of tanka, arranged in four sections: "earth," "wind," "fire," and "water." These elements are very important for the reader to understand the delicacy of insights within the poems. I try to give each poem a certain resonance. The weather is prominent throughout. The poems are lyrical, but the reader is expected to participate in the experience of the poems.

Laryea: I read somewhere that tanka is a Japanese form older than the recorded history of Japan. I've noticed how uniquely you pull experiences or images from the African American culture to record them in this ancient art form. For instance, you write:

> a day without wind—
> a fine evening rain hisses
> through yellow willows;

the teenager unbraiding
her grandma's thinning gray hair

and

Funeral Parlor:
a black man rolls the casket
down the crowded aisle,
little by little his shoes
shadow/shine in the white light

What makes these tanka?

Moore: Tanka is a five-line poem, consisting of thirty-one syllables. There are five syllables in the first line, seven in the second, five in the third, seven in the fourth, and seven in the fifth line. Many contemporary tanka poets use fewer syllables. Love is often the subject of a tanka, yet some include observations of the natural world and even a portrait of the poet. Tanka is serious in nature and incorporates a wealth of passion. In my tanka, I am constantly celebrating African American culture. That is what I live and know, the richness of my culture.

Laryea: I find the writing of renga to be especially fascinating too because it's a collaborative art form of linked verse with alternating stanzas that are composed by two or more poets. How do you choose a poet with whom you write renga?

Moore: I usually select a well-seasoned haiku poet to write a renga, or a well-known haiku poet might write or call me to write a renga.

Laryea: Who decides on the subject or theme, or do you both?

Moore: The poet who writes the hokku or first haiku in a renga really decides the topic. But there are several rules to consider, such as certain links or haiku must be about flowers, the moon, love, and so forth.

Laryea: So, the idea then is to link sequences and to evoke themes of love, the full moon, progress, and the seasons.

Moore: Yes. A renga must speed up as it progresses. At any rate, the poem must be tight. If there is repetition in a renga, it cannot happen too close to the previous links.

Laryea: When do you know a renga is finished?

Moore: Poets who write renga understand that there are a certain number of links that comprise the poem. I have been writing renga that consists of thirty-six links. However, a renga may consist of one hundred links.

Laryea: Are you aware of any other African American poets who write renga regularly? At all?

Moore: No, I'm not. I really would like to locate one.

Laryea: Most of your renga, like your haiku, are grounded in nature, I've noticed, with various allusions to your own cultural heritage. I really like the seriousness and the elegant style of "Snow in Stampede Pass" and "Beyond the Loon's Cry," but my favorite is "Even Bullfrogs Get the Blues," composed between May 1991 and November 1991. Maybe it's the title that grabs me, or the frogs themselves. They are the same ones I hear on my lake at night singing me to sleep. How did you compose it?

Moore: It took six months to write the poem. I wrote the renga with Lorraine Ellis Harr, a very famous American haiku poet. She also writes under the name Tombo. She has been writing haiku for more than thirty years. We sent each other links through the mail. So that is how we composed the renga. Some renga poets gather around a table for several hours to compose a renga, but Lorraine lives in Portland, Oregon, and I live in Raleigh, North Carolina. So, there was too much distance for us to write "Even Bullfrogs Get the Blues" in person together. Of course, we aimed to create a surprise ending to the poem, as all renga must have, for the conclusion. A renga must have an opening, development, and ending like any good song. I wrote the links while Lorraine wrote the haiku in "Even Bullfrogs Get the Blues." But usually, the haiku and links alternate between the poets.

Laryea: What do you try to do in your renga?

Moore: I ensure that there are twists and turns that will create a level of surprise. I try to make certain that the linking of the haiku is very smooth, too. I try to include fresh language and much imagery in my renga poems, and it is important that time progresses in a renga. So, I am very much aware of this time element. In some way, I aim to ensure the ending connects with the opening of the renga itself. That's the way the bullfrogs work in "Even Bullfrogs Get the Blues." Also, the reader can witness the phases of the moon in that particular renga poem.

Laryea: For three or four years now, you have been experimenting with another Japanese form called "haibun," a form I must admit I'd never heard of until I started reading your work. Define haibun and talk a little about it.

Moore: It is a short prose with haiku incorporated within the form. The prose and the haiku must be related in some way to deepen the effect of the haibun. A haibun opens with events that the author experiences day by day. The author uses such an economy of language to transcend his or her experience through haibun. Haibun is similar to keeping a diary. It works like an autobiography for me. It is important that precision is used when writing; however, the events must be recorded without sentimentality. Bashō wrote a number of important haibun in his lifetime. His work contains many allusions and demonstrates an appreciation for life. That is the way I hope my haibun unfolds. Moreover, I aim to create several layers of meaning, and irony is important in haibun. That's what I hope I have done in "In the Owl's Claws" and other haibun I have written.

Laryea: What else do you write?

Moore: I write free verse, blues poems, jazz poems, triolets, villanelles, twelve-tone poems, rondels, and so forth. I have written a few dramatic monologues, short stories, essays, book reviews, and autobiographical works. Just recently, I finished writing a play, and I've been working on a novel for several years now.

Laryea: Often a writer with this versatility of talent is better in one genre than others. How do you see yourself?

Moore: I see myself as an African American poet. I am primarily a poet, but I have had a great deal of success with my prose, too.

Laryea: Who are your literary role models?

Moore: Gwendolyn Brooks, August Wilson, Toni Morrison, Richard Wright, Rita Dove, and Langston Hughes, among others. I like the way Brooks writes about Black people, using language that is tight! I like the way she uses alliteration, too. Her poems are celebrations, and that is good. Wilson's work seems so real, and I know people who are like his characters. Morrison's fiction reads like poetry and incorporates so much history and folklore. Her narrators tell very memorable stories that are at once intense. I like the way Wright's fiction parallels race relations in America. I like the importance that geography plays in his fiction, too. His characters are so well developed that they take on real lives. That is important. Dove is an expert with imagery, and she knows how to narrate a story in her poetry. Her poetry demonstrates such control of language. She can write masterfully from a male's point of view as well as from a woman's point of view. Hughes's poetry sings about the common folk. I like the jazz in his poetry. His poems are very accessible. They will be around for a long time. They are so rich with symbolism and statement.

I think my work has begun to work on many different levels beyond the literal. I also find that I've been writing because I have to, not just because I want to. I revise my work endlessly. Then I ponder over it to rework it into art. It's important to me to use fresh language or originality. I feel that

I know what makes a poem work. I'm also able to sustain a theme more and more on African American culture in my writing, which I feel is important to my growth as a poet. So, I feel that my work is progressing in several ways.

Laryea: Let's talk about your reading performances. Each year you are invited to do a large number of poetry readings around the country. You have read at the Library of Congress, the National Black Arts Festival, the Walt Whitman Cultural Arts Center in Camden, New Jersey, and just recently you were one of eighty poets invited to read at Gwendolyn Brooks's eightieth birthday celebration in Chicago. I've attended several readings, and I've noticed how they attract a large audience. You read at museums, galleries, schools, colleges, universities, cultural centers, and the like. In a review of one of your readings sponsored by the North Carolina Writers' Network, Matthew Brennan wrote in *African American Review* that you "end every line with a rising inflection, a habit that particularly undermines the impressively *written* closure of several poems. . . ." He goes on to say that the fusion of your "unmodulated pitch and an excessive repetition of words . . . produces, for me, monotony more than jazz." He does highlight, however, the impressive quality of your poetry. Would you comment on Brennan's reaction to the reading?

Moore: It seems that Matthew Brennan gives good insight into my reading. But the way I read or perform my poems depends upon the type of poem it is. The video that he reviewed includes primarily blues poems and jazz poems. So naturally, I would read them quite differently from the way that I would read other types of poetry. I love jazz, and when I read my jazz poems, I become an instrument. I listen to it almost every day. I love blues and soul, too. So, these kinds of music influence me to write poetry. I like the rhythms, innovations, intonations, repetitions, and emotional impact of the music. My poem "A Poem for Langston Hughes" includes these elements as well as several literary elements. The poem is very musical and alludes to themes that Hughes dealt with in his poetry. It celebrates the way my people walk and talk within its jazz rhythm. The reading of such a poem demands that I bear in mind what I am trying to do here.

Laryea: Let me now turn to the Carolina African American Writers' Collective, a group you have founded and of which you serve as executive director. What led you to begin this group, and what are its purpose and composition?

Moore: I am really glad you want to talk about this group. I began it because I knew that African American writers needed a forum to discuss works in progress and stay abreast of the literary market. For the last sixteen years, I have been the only African American at many literary gatherings in North Carolina. At times, Jaki Shelton Green would be in attendance. Many African Americans work in isolation, yet in the mid-1980s Jaki Green, Kristi Mullen [Harryette Mullen's sister], and I met to discuss various issues that concerned African Americans. Then I met Janice Hodges in January of 1989. We took an advanced poetry-writing class together. I kept telling Janice that I was going to start a writers' group. Finally, on February 9, 1992, I sent a letter to Jaki, Janice, Carole Boston Weatherford, Cynthia Guinn, and Beverly Fields Burnette. The group struggled with its membership at first. Beverly was the only person who attended meetings in the beginning stages. So, I would provide one-on-one critiques of her poetry. The purpose of the group is to provide critiques of members' literary works, to study African American literature, to share literary market news, and to read collectively at literary programs and conferences. The composition of the collective includes twenty women and ten men. Their ages range from seventeen to sixty-five. The group meets once a month at my house. The meetings usually start at 2:00 p.m. on Saturdays because we have members who drive from Virginia. Others drive from South Carolina and Ohio.

Laryea: Has the group gotten good results?

Moore: Yes, I feel we have gotten great results. We have published in *Fertile Ground* and *Dark Eros*. Some members were published in *African American Review, Obsidian II, Nu Voices, Drumvoices Revue,* and so forth. Several of the members will be appearing in the anthology *Beyond the Frontier*. We have read collectively at libraries, bookstores, and the Page One Festival of the Books. Certainly, our members are part of this new artistic Black Renaissance. For example, Gaye L. Newton and Bridgette A. Lacy have signed on with agents to market their novels. Victor E. Blue and Lana C. Williams are publishing essays in the *Independent Weekly* and elsewhere. Honoree F. Jeffers, Christopher Stanard, and Janice W. Hodges are publishing poetry everywhere. In addition, Beverly Fields Burnette, Carole Boston Weatherford, and Oktavi are publishing powerful poems. L. Teresa Church is very strong in prose and poetry. She is an awesome playwright, too. Patricia A. Johnson is a strong reader/performer. Her poetry is good, too. These are the writers to watch during the next decade. But Wendell W. Ottley III, Estelle E. Farley, Darrell Stover, Paula White-Jackson, Daniel J. Wideman [John Edgar Wideman's son], and Takea will be making their marks on the literary world, too. Carole has already published memorable poems. Rebecca Lynn Delbridge [Oktavi's daughter], a recent high school graduate, however, shows much promise in her work. Brian H. Jackson and Vickie Stanford show promise, too. Last year, I received a 1996 Indies Arts Award for my work with the Carolina African American Writers' Collective.

Laryea: So, you are part of a new Black literary renaissance?

Moore: There is definitely a new Black renaissance of the 1990s that is redefining American literature. This current renaissance is so full of fire, lyricism, symbolism, and innovation of language and form that publishers are publishing African American writers as fast as we can create our literary works. Hip-hop artists are very much a part of this new wave of literature. However, this Renaissance is not happening in just one particular section of the country. African American writers are giving literature a voice everywhere: Raleigh, Durham, Charlotte, Atlanta, St. Louis, Chicago, Los Angeles, Philadelphia, Washington, DC, New York, Baltimore, Detroit, Newark, and on and on. Some of the poets who have emerged from this are Elizabeth Alexander, Carl Phillips, Sharon Strange, Paul Beatty, Sapphire, Charlie Braxton, Patricia Spears Jones, Allison Joseph, Kevin Powell, Thomas Sayers Ellis, Patricia Smith, and Kevin Young. So, whenever critics examine this current 1990s renaissance, they must consider these poets.

Laryea: What are we to expect in the future?

Moore: Well, I have finished a manuscript of revelations, reflecting upon the Million Man March. The poem is a book-length one, and I call it *A Million Shadows at Noon*. What I try to do in this poem is to express a magnitude of hope for the African American male. It aims to make sense of the Million Man March by capturing the images and sounds of the event. It offers a stark contrast between autumn and the march. The introduction to this book has been written by Jerry W. Ward Jr., and the afterword has been written by E. Ethelbert Miller. I feel good about their statements about the book. It should be coming out soon. Then too, you can expect to see a manuscript called *A Temple Looming: Photographic Memory*. It is a collection of poems based on old photographs of African Americans that were taken at the turn of the century. Some of them may have been taken in the 1920s. I got the photographs from Sherman Jenkins, an emerging African American photographer living in Raleigh. The poems in this collection consist of a variety of forms: free verse, blank verse, dramatic monologues, haiku, tanka, and formal verse. Highly imaginative, *A Temple Looming: Photographic Memory* is an ambitious manuscript of observations that include a deep sense of mystery. I wanted the poems to be as visually pleasing as the photographs. The work is divided into four parts. Each provides certain music, yet I try to portray the people as gracefully as possible. I hope this will be a memorable collection and will evoke enduring emotions within the reader. I feel good about these poems and really enjoyed writing them. Readers can expect to see more of my jazz and blues poems. I will continue to write as long as I have the spark. It's my lifeblood.

On Being and Becoming a Writer: Interview with Lenard D. Moore

L. Teresa Church / 2009

From *Obsidian: Literature in the African Diaspora* 10, no. 2 (2009): 129–42. Reprinted by permission.

Jacksonville, North Carolina, native Lenard D. Moore is a writer of great passion. His name is synonymous with poetry. He speaks in the tongues of sonnets, pantoums, ghazals, sestinas, villanelles, free verse, blues and jazz poems, haiku, senryu, minutes, kwansabas, and other forms. Moore is known in literary circles throughout his home state and across the United States, as well as in several other countries. He is the founder and executive director of the Carolina African American Writers' Collective and cofounder of the Washington Street Writers Group. His poems, essays, and reviews have appeared in over thirty publications, such as *Agni, Callaloo, African American Review, Colorado Review, North Dakota Quarterly, Obsidian II,* and *Poetry Canada Review*. His poetry is featured in more than thirty anthologies and has been translated into several languages. Moore is the author of *The Open Eye, Forever Home,* and *Desert Storm: A Brief History*. Praises and recognition have come in abundance, yet he remains humble and accessible, eager to talk about writing and what it means to become a writer. During the spring of 2004, he sat down with poet and playwright L. Teresa Church to talk about his illustrious career.

L. Teresa Church: How did you come to the craft of writing, and what influenced you to become a writer?

Lenard D. Moore: I believe that was a long process that started when I was in elementary school. While riding the bus to Silverdale Elementary School [in Jacksonville, North Carolina] I read books oftentimes. In those books, I noticed that I could go places. I liked the way that kind of worked my imagination, so I had a love of words early on. Also, my grandfather, Luther T. Pearson Sr., told lots of stories. My brothers, sister, and I gathered around him and listened to the rich stories he told us. That was inspiring, and I had very good elementary school teachers. This was during segregation—segregated times—at an all-Black school like the one where I'm sure you attended. I participated in plays, dramas if you will. All those things were exciting. I wrote some plays, too, when I was little, and I participated in plays at church and in church programs. I think all of that was very important.

My teacher in seventh grade assigned us to write a play, and mine was one of the ones selected for staging. I don't want to use the word *produced* because in the classroom you're just putting the play on for other students or classmates. Some of my classmates and I were in my play. That was fun and encouraging. In tenth grade, we wrote some short stories, and that, too, was encouraging. I remember that I enjoyed writing those stories. In fact, two of my stories were science fiction, and I tried to depict some of my classmates in some of those stories.

I kept, I guess you would call it, a journal, but our teacher also had us keep a diary when we were in tenth grade. I wrote words down, song titles, names for our dance group, and just different things. I always loved words. I wrote poems too. When I was twenty, I believe I had a major turning point. I went to the army, and while there, I wrote a lot of poems. I was sending poems back home. First, I was trying to write letters in poetic form and send them to my girlfriend [Lynn, who is now his wife]. Not long afterward, I started to include a poem with each letter, then maybe sometimes two. Lynn has kept those poems ever since. They're sort of brown now; the paper has faded a little bit, but she still has poems in my handwriting.

LTC: Do you share those poems?

LDM: Not really. When I was starting out, they were not that good. Maybe they were to Lynn, but now that I've been writing awhile, I realize the craft was not quite there yet.

LTC: You were getting started.

LDM: I was getting started. Right.

LTC: You said that you started writing in elementary school. How old were you when you actually penned your first poem?

LDM: I don't believe I remember the exact age that I might have been at that time. I went home a few months ago, and while at church, one of my homegirls, who graduated two years before I did, told me she remembered that I wrote poems when I was young, perhaps at some of the church programs, or something. I don't believe I really recall the very first time that I did write a poem, but I do know that I had a love of words. I still have a love of words. In fact, while in the army, I would read the dictionary. Really, I believe in learning new words. When I write, I usually have the dictionary right there with me—the dictionary and a good thesaurus. I believe in the power of words.

LTC: You grew up in Jacksonville. Is that a farming country, and was your family involved with farming?

LDM: Jacksonville, since about the early 1940s, is a military community. Here in the twenty-first century, like everywhere else, the landscape has changed, with strip malls and all of that. There were many farms in the area. White people had farms. Black people had farms. My great-grandmother, Fannie Simmons, had a lot of land, and she had two huge fields and grew peanuts every year. Two of my brothers and I would chop in her peanut fields with her. At that time, she was about eighty years old. We also farmed with other people who owned tobacco fields. I did a lot of gardening every year, and I had a huge garden myself.

LTC: What did your family do to make a living in Jacksonville?

LDM: Jacksonville was very rural. My father was in the marine corps, and my mother started out doing volunteer work with the American Red Cross. Then, she got a job at Camp Lejeune, working in the club system, until she worked her way up to become a supervisor in the club system.

LTC: What do you mean when you say "the club system?"

LDM: That's like the NGO Club, where the troops, or the marines, go to have lunch, or maybe at night they want to hear some music.

LTC: With the kind of childhood you had, did you stand apart, as a child who was interested in writing? Was that so different between your childhood and that of other children?

LDM: I'm not sure whether I stood apart, but I know I tried to do my homework and make good grades. I don't recall any other people in the area who had an interest in writing poetry. Years later, I found out that my grandmother, Eva Pearson, who died on March 9, 2004, wrote poetry. In recent years, she shared some of her poetry with me, but I don't recall anyone whom I knew at the time writing or publishing poetry. I can't say there were any poets in that area. However, we know that in every community there are always people writing and, perhaps, they don't show their works or poems to others for whatever reason.

LTC: When I think about you as a poet, I never find you without a pen or a piece of paper on which you jot down something about the surroundings in which you find yourself. Why do you do that?

LDM: One reason is to hopefully make sense of the world in which we live and to learn something about myself. I find out things about myself through my own writing. When I write, I find that I can create the world that I want to exist in. I think that's fun. Also, I hope to record our history and our experiences and write about the truth.

LTC: Do you write every day?

LDM: I try to write something every day. Sometimes I may write haiku for several days. Then, there are times when I may write tanka. There are other times when I'm on a roll with a free verse or some other form of poetry. Sometimes, I may work on an essay and then occasionally work on fiction or creative nonfiction. Some days when I don't get a chance to write, I may read.

LTC: How important is reading to you as a writer?

LDM: Reading is very important because as a writer I must be aware of others who have written, who have left us a body of work, who have in some way or other defined the world in which they lived at that time. I read to hopefully understand the tradition, which is so important.

LTC: Who are some of your favorite authors, and who has been influential in your own work?

LDM: Langston Hughes is one of those influential writers whom I read quite often, and I also share his works with my students. I like the way that he wrote about the African American experience and the way that he used blues as a form for his poetry and the way that he used jazz as well, to pen his poems. Hughes was heavily influenced by music, and I, too, listen to jazz quite frequently, live jazz, as well as jazz recordings, or jazz on the radio. I think that has influenced my work. Langston Hughes is one of those very important writers to me. Gwendolyn Brooks was also very important and still is in my writing life. I like the way she wrote about the people she knew in Chicago, giving them a voice when many times others wouldn't let those folks' voices speak. I like the economy of words that Brooks used. I also like A. R. Ammons's work. He wrote a lot about nature and a lot about North Carolina, so I feel that I'm able to identify with the geography, which he wrote about in his poems.

LTC: Tell me what your writing process is like.

LDM: I write in my journal, and sometimes I write on loose sheets of paper. A line may come to me, and I may start writing a poem, and it seems that I never know where the poem is going to take me, where the poem is going to turn, where the poem might take some leap, or where the poem might try to draw some parallels, where it might hook some interesting idea that I didn't think about when I first started writing the poem, or where the poem may end up.

LTC: You write in a variety of forms, including tanka and haiku. How did you come to be attracted to these forms?

LDM: It is very interesting how I came to haiku. In January of 1982, I was in bed sick with the flu. When you have the flu you're down for a while, and I suppose I had gotten a little bored and wanted to do something. I looked at my literature book that I had used in a creative-writing class that I took when I was stationed in Stuttgart, Germany. In that book, I noticed there were haiku translated from Japanese into English, so I tried writing some haiku, very unsuccessful attempts at first, but I didn't give up. That's how I first became aware of haiku. I didn't know anything about the form. I thought it was just these little poems composed of three lines, but that was definitely not the case. That's not what haiku is.

LTC: You have become very well known, nationally and internationally, as a haiku poet. What does that mean for you as a writer?

LDM: It means that I must try to work harder and try to refine my craft even more. Hopefully, it means that haiku helps with my other forms of writing. I believe it does help, especially with free verse, being able to chisel a poem until it's tight as a rubber band. When a poem is tight like that, hopefully, it will sing to my reader and convey a message that somehow will move the reader. I hope the reader will find some connection with his or her life through reading that work.

LTC: What are some of the awards you have won as a haiku poet?

LDM: I've been blessed with winning the Haiku Museum of Literature Award on three different occasions. When I first received that award, I believe it was called the Haiku Museum of Tokyo Award. I was awarded that prize in 1983, again in 1994, and most recently toward the end of 2003.

LTC: What does it mean for you to be kind of out there by yourself if you will, and so well-known for what you do as an African American who writes haiku so successfully?

LDM: Well, as Robert Frost's famous poem has illustrated to us, or as so many people have quoted, about "taking the path less traveled," I hope that's what I'm doing and trying to create a path for other African Americans who might attempt to write haiku. I'm not the first African American to write haiku, however. Richard Wright wrote many haiku. In fact, there is a book of his haiku entitled *Haiku: This Other World*. Sonia Sanchez has also been writing haiku for decades. She has written tanka and other forms, too. Kalamu ya Salaam writes haiku and has been doing so for a while. Etheridge

Knight also wrote haiku. I believe, however, that the mainstream is mostly aware of Richard Wright and Etheridge Knight's haiku. I've been working in—I guess you would call it the haiku community—for a long time, and I believe that for a long time I was the only African American working in that community.

When I say haiku community, I'm referring to the haiku organizations that are in this country and elsewhere. Some examples are the Haiku Society of America and the North Carolina Haiku Society, of which I am the executive chairman. There are also other haiku organizations and haiku magazines, including *Frogpond, Modern Haiku,* and the *Heron's Nest,* where my work has been published. Early on, a couple of decades ago, my work was also published in *Dragonfly* and *Wind Chimes* and some other haiku magazines and in a number of haiku journals in foreign countries. At that time, I believe I was the only African American doing that. However, Francis Alexander is an African American who has also become known in the haiku community in recent years.

LTC: How does tanka differ from haiku?

LDM: Tanka differs from haiku in that it is a poem that usually has five lines and seems to be an extension of haiku. Many people might say that a tanka has five, seven, five, seven, seven syllables. However, I don't believe contemporary tanka adheres to those strict syllables. A tanka is usually about love or relationships and may, or may not, have a kigo in it. Tanka is probably also more musical than haiku because you have more space there in which to create that music.

LTC: What is a kigo?

LDM: *Kigo* is a Japanese word that means season word, and a season word informs the reader as to which season that poem may be depicting.

LTC: Have you taken classes dealing with these poetic forms?

LDM: No, I haven't taken any classes in those forms. I've read a lot, and I've written a lot, so I think the best thing to do is read and also write as often as possible and then try your hand at submitting some of the poems and see what happens.

LTC: Have you received awards for your tanka poetry?

LDM: Yes, I entered the 1994 Tanka Splendor contest, and my poem "glowing moon" was a finalist. That poem was published in the 1994 Tanka Splendor Awards chapbook, and it was reprinted in the anthology *Full Moon Tide* in 2000. Jane Reichhold created the award and sponsored the competition.

LTC: What are some of the other Japanese forms that you write in, and what do they entail?

LDM: I've also written renga, and that's a poem in which you write with other haiku poets. One person may write a haiku, or that first haiku—the opening haiku called a *hokku*. Oftentimes the title of the entire renga comes from a line in the *hokku*. Then, another person writes a link—two lines, and then a haiku, and it moves on. There are different links. At that time, I was writing renga, that form consisted of thirty-six links. Recently, I've been writing renku. That too is a poem where you have more than one person participating—one person writing a haiku, another writing a link, followed by another haiku. Then, there are certain subjects that should be included in different links: maybe flowers in a link, the moon in a link, love in a link, just different things. There are different types of renku, too. In fact, a twenty-link renku is called a *nijuin*. Also, there is a twelve-stanza renku or twelve-link renku, and that's called a *shisan*. Certain links should be about summer, or no season, or certain ones about autumn or autumn moon. There are lots of rules you have to follow when writing these poems. In the twenty-link, or twenty-stanza renku, the last one is the ageku. That's the end of the poem. There are a number of elements that must be in there. I really enjoy writing those forms. You really have to work hard when writing renku, and you usually have a renku master who is leading the renku session or renku party. Oftentimes, the participants, or the writers, will have to go back and rewrite until the poem is right—until it fits. There must be some linking. You can't just have a poem there. They must connect; there must be some link, and there must be some shifts.

LTC: Okay. What is a haibun?

LDM: Haibun is another Japanese form, and it consists of prose and poetry. The prose is almost like journal writing, and it is poetic, or rhythmical, and has lots of imagery. Then there is a haiku, or maybe the prose is longer with haiku interspersed throughout. Sometimes, it may end with a haiku. So, haibun is prose and poetry or prose and haiku.

LTC: How many Japanese forms are you proficient at writing?

LDM: I'm not exactly certain. At one time I was writing in more than a dozen Japanese forms. In the early 1980s, for example, I wrote senka. I wrote Japanese octaves (consisting of eight lines) and senryu, which people will say is the opposite of haiku, in that it is about human nature and usually humorous. That's the difference between senryu and haiku.

LTC: How did you get started writing blues and jazz poems?

LDM: With my blues poems, I mentioned early on that I read Langston Hughes's poems, you know, in *The Weary Blues*. I read Raymond Patterson's poetry, and he wrote a lot of blues poetry. Also, Sterling Plumpp wrote a lot of blues poetry—and still does. I've listened to blues music or blues songs. I realize that you have to feel the blues to be able to write about the blues. You have to experience some pain or something so that you can be able to write about the blues and hopefully overcome whatever that pain might be or whatever caused that pain. I listen to a lot of blues music and blues musicians. I read a lot of blues poetry and pay attention to structure. Usually, somebody has lost something, or something isn't going right—lost their woman, lost their man. Something has happened, and they're trying to overcome that, so, I'm trying to write through that experience with the blues poems.

LTC: Are there particular blues musicians that have been influential in your writing of blues poems?

LDM: Well, early on I was listening to B.B. King. His music reached mainstream culture more, so I was able to listen to his music back when I was growing up and as a teenager. Perhaps Denise LaSalle is also considered a blues artist. At least, that's what I thought she was singing when I used to listen to her music early on. Then, of course, there is Koko Taylor. These are some of the blues artists whom I've been influenced by in one way or another, through listening to their music or listening to their stories and trying to figure out what they were writing about, what their pains were, what caused them to write that, or what was the impulse for that work. Hopefully, I am able to do that through my own experience.

LTC: How does jazz poetry differ from blues poetry?

LDM: Jazz poetry is much more upbeat than blues poetry. There have been lots of African American poets writing about jazz, as well as prose writers who have been writing about jazz and blues or blues and jazz. One you might think about is Albert Murray. If you talk about jazz poetry, you have to mention Michael S. Harper. His book, *Dear John, Dear Coltrane*, was published, I believe, in 1970. That is an excellent model for someone who wants to study jazz poetry. I say study because you must read and study whatever you want to write. If it's poetry, you must study good poetry, and you must learn the tradition. If it's fiction, you must study fiction—read. Learn the tradition and see how each element works in that story. See what makes the poem work, see how that poet uses metaphor, see how that poet bends the language and incorporates current events into his or her work. There are lots of things you must learn when trying to develop your own craft. Those are some of the things I try to do myself. Read as often as possible. Study, study, and write, and, of course, experience jazz. I go to lots of jazz performances and listen to jazz artists—live jazz and recorded jazz. I've also read some of my poetry with jazz artists in Ohio, in New York, and all around. I'm always reading about jazz. I'm always listening to jazz. Then, I feel that you have an ear for the language. I hope that's what is happening with my work.

LTC: Who are some of the people that have mentored you in your study of poetry?

LDM: I believe the main poet whom I've studied with is Gerald W. Barrax. I say that because, in 1988, I took a beginning poetry-writing class with him at North Carolina State University. Then, in 1989, I took his advanced poetry-writing class. In that class, that's where I met Janice W. Hodges who is a member of the Carolina African American Writers' Collective, the organization to which you and I belong and where we write and share our poetry with others. Later, during the spring semester of 1992, I took the graduate poetry-writing workshop with Gerald Barrax. He has been an influence on the way that I revise my work, the way that I look at my work certainly. I've learned a lot from him in that respect. The only other class that I took was a creative-writing class, and I believe that was during the spring of 1981 when I was stationed in Stuttgart, Germany. This class was taught through the University of Maryland Overseas Branch. There was a Black lady in that class with me. I think she and I were the only two Black students in that class. I was in my very early twenties at the time, and she might have been in her late thirties or early forties—I'm not sure. I remember her saying in that class that "Gwendolyn Brooks is my favorite poet." At that time, I didn't know who Gwendolyn Brooks was, so that sent me on a journey to find out more about her. That was a class where we basically studied poetry, although we did write some poems, too.

LTC: In addition to the various courses you took while serving in the military, you have an undergraduate degree from Shaw University. What did you study there?

LDM: At Shaw, I took literature classes as well as business classes. My major was liberal studies with a minor in English. I did quite well and won a trophy for my area of studies, as the top student. I studied a wide range of liberal arts, reading about Aristotle, Plato, and others.

LTC: You also have a master's degree in African American literature from North Carolina A&T State University. What was your objective in pursuing a degree in that field?

LDM: I wanted to know even more about African American literature, although many of those people whom we studied I had already read. In the graduate program, we got into a deeper study of those authors' works, and so forth. I really enjoyed reading Toni Morrison, Zora Neale Hurston, and James Baldwin and studying their novels, not just their short stories. We looked at the various movements in African American poetry in the African American poetry class. I enjoyed all of that, and I think it was important, as well as writing long papers on particular writers. That helped my critical skills, as far as writing criticism and thinking about literature. That's what I gained from the graduate program and through earning my degree in African American literature.

LTC: We have talked about your work as a student of literature, but how does your career differ when you take to the other side of the table as a teacher of writing and of literature?

LDM: As a teacher, I hope that by the end of the semester, my students will come away from the class being more aware of writers—African American writers and the African American experience. I hope they will have an awareness of what was happening at a particular time in African American culture. They will get that in their writings and know more about African American history. They will understand more about the African American family, religion—all of those things—it's all in there. Also, they will understand something about the literary tradition. If you're going to write, you have to understand the classics and other works that have gone on before you even existed. That's so important, and I hope that my students are able to get a sense of themselves through reading that work. Hopefully, they will look at the world in a new light after having studied the literature, or humanities, which I also teach. It's very important for them to see that all of the arts relate in some way or another and how all of the arts attempt to define the world in which we live, how all of the arts try to say something about society, how all of the arts try to make some kind of political statement, how all of the arts try to leave something of permanence about a particular period. I hope that I'm able to convey all of that and that my students will leave those classes wanting to read more.

LTC: Where have you taught?

LDM: I've been teaching in the schools for a couple of decades as a writer-in-residence, or poet in the schools, going into different schools and teaching poetry. When I was in San Diego from 1983 to 1984, I was a writer-in-residence at the Mira Mesa Branch Library, and I taught some workshops for the community and some children's workshops—poetry workshops. Just before I left, I had been accepted to teach in the California Poets in the Schools program. Not long after I received the acceptance letter, I decided to come back to North Carolina, where I also worked in the schools. I was a high school English teacher for a year. I started, for a couple of months, teaching a creative-writing class at Enloe High School in Raleigh, North Carolina, but a teacher left, and I was moved in to teach her classes. There, I taught ninth-grade English.

Then, I went on to attend graduate school at North Carolina A&T State University. As a grad student there, I was also a graduate teaching assistant. I say assistant, but I taught the classes. I taught English and worked on the staff of the literary magazine *All That Jazz*. After finishing the program at North Carolina A&T, I taught at North Carolina State University where I taught composition. I also taught studies in modern poetry and poetry writing at North Carolina State University. I taught there from August 1997 until January 1, 2001.

Then, I came to Shaw University and began teaching world literature, humanities, and a couple of writing courses. I enjoy teaching and feel that teaching helps my own writing. Teaching helps me to stay abreast of things. I read a lot of criticism and I read a lot of other writers. Teaching really helps to sharpen the teacher's or the professor's thinking, writing, and all those skills. I feel that teaching is a mutual experience. More so than the professor giving, the students should be giving, too. That's when I think you have the best experience.

LTC: What year did you get your degree from North Carolina A&T State University?

LDM: I finished the program in August of 1997, but I didn't walk across the stage until May of 1998.

LTC: When did you graduate from Shaw University, as an undergraduate?

LDM: I graduated from Shaw University in 1995. However, I had been going to school for a while, off and on, I first started at Coastal Carolina Community College in 1976, but in 1978, I left and went to the army. I took classes in the army, too. I could only take one class per semester. As you know, taking one class at a time takes a long time to finish. I also took classes at North Carolina State University.

LTC: With your love for the land and your family in North Carolina, how did you come to find yourself living in California?

LDM: My wife is from California. She's from San Diego, and I was out there. It's a different terrain. I didn't see any farms or anything like that out there, so I feel that I was able to write a different kind of poetry at that time. I believe I wrote my poem "A Poem for Langston Hughes" when I was out in San Diego, and that poem will tell you that that is a different type of poetry from the poems that are in my book *Forever Home*. While living in

California, I believe that is when I had some major publications of my work. *Stepping Stones* magazine accepted my poem entitled "A Poem for Langston Hughes." Another poem that I had written in San Diego was accepted for publication in *Kansas Quarterly*, and I was very excited about that. I also had a poem published in *AIM*, which I believe came out of Chicago at that time, and that was the first time I had received a check for a poem.

LTC: What exactly did you go to California seeking?

LDM: I went out there to join my wife and daughter. I went there, too, for employment opportunities and to write and to get into the literary scene out there. I went to lots of readings out in California and read at a lot of places, too. I feel that was an important place for my development, an important place for my experimentation, an important place for my working more deeply into poetic language.

LTC: How long did you stay in San Diego?

LDM: I was out there from June 1983 to January 1984.

LTC: Why did you return to North Carolina?

LDM: North Carolina is home. What is the title of my book? *Forever Home*, and the opening poem in that book is "The Homeplace."

LTC: You have done tremendous work in North Carolina, as a writer, working with writers' groups and serving on panels. How has this service impacted your career as a writer?

LDM: I feel that is important work to do. As a writer, I feel that we should give back to the community, especially if we have some expertise that we have gained through experience, particularly if we want to be an advocate for the literary arts. I feel that we should participate on boards or committees that request us to help make the climate better, if you will, for literary artists or writers.

LTC: How did you conceive the idea of starting the Carolina African American Writers' Collective?

LDM: Wow, you see I'm smiling when you mention the Carolina African American Writers' Collective. You know how much I love that organization. Well, I've already mentioned that I took an advanced poetry-writing class with Gerald Barrax at North Carolina State University, and I have already mentioned that Janice Hodges was one of my classmates. Janice and I were the only two African American poets in that class. There were times when she and I had to explain certain things in our poems that dealt with our culture or Black culture. I feel that it takes a lot of time away from explicating a poem, critiquing a poem, or offering valuable comments or feedback if you have to do all this preliminary work. Now, that didn't happen every time, but there were times when we had to explain certain things in our poems. I remember telling Janice that I was thinking about starting a group, a writing group for African American poets, where we could come together to discuss literature, discuss creative writing, or our poetry, and, of course, study other authors and study Black writing and Black writers. I feel that is so important because we need to be in touch with our ancestors, to be in touch with our people who have gone before us and who wrote such marvelous literary works.

LTC: What do you think is the success of the Carolina African American Writers' Collective, or "The Collective," as we call it?

LDM: I think one of the major successes of the Collective is that through the past decade I have been able to see significant growth in the works of our members. I think that is very important, and I feel great about that. That's one of the major accomplishments of the group. Another thing I think very important is that the group has been together for so long because many groups don't stay together for that long. I think that is a major accomplishment in itself.

Also, to go on the road and read at different venues—that's a great thing. We've done that several times at venues such as the Virginia Festival of the Book, the North Carolina Literary Festival, the National Black Arts Festival, the Bimbé Festival [in Durham, North Carolina], the Festival for the Eno [also in Durham, North Carolina], as well as a lot of colleges, including the Mount Olive College Literary Festival. We've read at a lot of places. We've read as a group, as the Carolina African American Writers' Collective, and I think that says a lot about our members' works. Hopefully, we're at a point where we will continue to publish as a group, and we've done that a lot also. We've been featured in several magazines and anthologies as a group, so I feel good about that. I think that is a major accomplishment. But I'm most proud of the growth of our members, as well as yours and mine.

LTC: How did you go about the process of soliciting members for the Carolina African American Writers' Collective? How did you get the word out and tell people to come and bring good work?

LDM: In February of 1992, I wrote a letter and addressed it to some of the writers in North Carolina, such as Jaki Shelton Green, Beverly Fields Burnette, and a few others. I informed them that I was starting a writing group and invited them to join. That's how it initially came about. Janice Hodges was one of those writers, too, and so was Cynthia Guinn, another writer who lived in Raleigh at that time. I sent out the initial letter, and for a while, Beverly Fields Burnette and I would meet at my house, and it was basically one-on-one because many people didn't show up in the beginning. Then, there was a major turning point when Lana G. Williams [now Afefe Tyehimba] called me one night, informing me that she had met Janice Hodges. Janice gave her my number and told her she might want to give me a call. Lana and I talked about her writing, and Black writing in general, and I remember her saying, "The time is now." So, I went at it again and sent out another letter [of invitation], and since that time, the Carolina African American Writers' Collective has been going strong. As you know, for the first several years of the organization, I would work on the newsletter: write it, type it up on my typewriter, include information about markets—literary markets, literary events, news about important books that were being published, news about our members—and distribute those newsletters at our meetings/workshops and also mail them to other writers, scholars, and teachers throughout the country as well as other countries. I just love the meetings when we gather—the Carolina African American Writers' Collective—we're like a family, one big family.

LTC: You said there was a turning point in 1995. What do you think that turning point was, or can you identify it?

LDM: I think there were more writers in the area at the time who were really serious about writing and who were looking for a gathering such as the Collective. I remember speaking with Victor E. Blue, who passed away in 2002, and he was serious. Also, I remember Cherry Floyd-Miller speaking with me, having an interest in the group, joining early on, and coming to the meetings. I believe she had read an article that I had written for the *Network News* [a publication of the North Carolina Writers Network], and from that point, she knew about my work and me. I believe writers were telling other writers about the meetings. That's how I believe the Collective got off the ground.

LTC: The first time I met you was when we read at Ravena's Coffeehouse in Durham. That was my first public reading, and the impression I got about you was that you were very much interested in writers, what writers were writing about, and what they were saying in their work. You were very cordial and very welcoming upon that first meeting. What is it that that kind of exchange gives you, and what do you hope to give in such an exchange in meeting new writers and writers in general?

LDM: I hope to be able to inspire, inform, and help writers to connect with other writers and to expand the literary community. If I remember correctly, I believe I gave you one of my business cards at that meeting, letting you know about the Carolina African American Writers' Collective. And from that point on, you've been a valuable member.

LTC: How did you become involved with the Washington Street Writers Group, of which you're also a member?

LDM: The way the Washington Street Writers Group came into existence—again, I must mention Gerald W. Barrax because I was taking the graduate poetry-writing workshop, and I met Bruce Lader who was one of my classmates. After the semester had ended, Bruce and I decided to start the Washington Street Writers Group. We've been meeting since July 1992. Unlike the Collective, which takes a summer break, the Washington Street Writers Group does not take a break; it meets year-round. We have members in this group such as Richard Krawiec, Sally Ann Drucker, Jan Hilton, Randy Pait, Beverly Fields Burnette, and Bruce Lader and his wife Renata Lader. We have a number of writers, and we have had other writers who were in the group but moved on or moved elsewhere out of the area. We meet to critique each other's work—poetry and fiction—just like we do in the Collective.

LTC: Now that you can look back over this long history of your involvement with writing, teaching writing, and studying writing, what are your goals for the future? What do you see yourself doing in five years, or ten years, or even twenty years from now, as a writer?

LDM: Hopefully, find more time to write and, of course, teach poetry and literature. I love teaching. I would like to give advice to younger writers, and that is to please study and read the literature as often as possible if they want to become writers. Then write, keep a journal, study the craft, and learn to write in forms.

A Haiku Consciousness:
An Interview with Lenard D. Moore

Sheila Smith McKoy / 2011

Printed by permission of Sheila Smith McKoy.

I had the pleasure of sitting with Lenard Moore on November 19, 2011, and again on September 29, 2013, to discuss his life and his work.

Sheila Smith McKoy: I'm here at Cameron Village Regional Library with Lenard D. Moore, one of my favorite haiku writers, and we've met today to talk about Lenard's work and actually the inspiring way that he's touched others with his art. How are you today, Lenard?
Lenard D. Moore: I'm fine. How are you? Wow, thanks for asking me to do this interview.
SSM: At your favorite place, the Cameron Village Regional Library.
LDM: I'm here all the time, grading papers, writing, whatever.
SSM: Your space, so I was just wondering which one out of all your books is your favorite?
LDM: That's a hard question! I really like that first book, you know. The first haiku book was, of course, *The Open Eye*. I was so excited when that work came out, but you know what, you're excited when any book comes out, especially *Desert Storm: A Brief History*. I tried to do a lot with that book. For one thing, that book is a sequence of haiku. So, hopefully, it will be read as one long poem. In that book I was trying to deal with history as well as with the natural world and a lot of other elements. So, that book took more time. And, hopefully, I was able to get that book right.
SSM: So, you're one of the few people who have blended issues of race, nature, and war with haiku. Tell me what that means for you.
LDM: I don't remember seeing anyone else doing that kind of work. I refuse to hide who I am, my whole identity. So, I tried to find a way to

incorporate all those elements into my work. I think it is very important, not only who I am, but also my affinity for the natural world. As you know, I grew up doing a lot of farm work; I feel a kinship with the earth. I think that also drove me to haiku. I wanted to find ways to experiment with haiku that I had not seen before.

SSM: So, we've talked a lot about your early upbringing working on farms in eastern North Carolina. How are you now inspired by nature differently than you were when you were beginning to write haiku?

LDM: I think particularly with haiku, that one is more attuned to nature or to the natural world. At least in my case, that's true. One of my books is titled *The Open Eye*. I feel that my eyes are opened to the natural world and, hopefully, my ears are more attuned to what might be happening in the natural world. I try to bring all that together and then include some other iconography that I didn't often see in haiku. For example, I've written some haiku about jazz; maybe you want to call it jazz haiku or jazzku. I don't know what you want to call it, but how could one not include his or her culture in his or her work? So, you know, music is prominent in African American and southern cultures: jazz, blues, spirituals, and other musical art forms. I try to get all those musical forms in my haiku.

SSM: Lenard, you have changed haiku, and, arguably, haiku has changed you. Take both prongs of that sentence and tell me: How have you changed haiku, and how has haiku changed you? Your view of the natural world is heightened by your experience with haiku. You are one of the few people that I know of American and African descent who has won major awards for your haiku.

LDM: Ahh, that's interesting that you say that. It has changed me. As I said, I feel that I'm more attuned to my natural surroundings and to the world itself. As my wife, Lynn, and I were traveling this past weekend, she was talking about how the leaves down in South Carolina aren't as vibrant as the ones here in North Carolina, and I told her perhaps it was the heat. I remember when I was at Fort Jackson for basic training, it was the middle of August, and it was very hot. So, maybe that had something to do with it, I don't know, but certainly I've noticed the leaves here are very colorful.

However, I think one thing that haiku has done is that it also helps one to appreciate nature more so than he or she may have before coming to haiku. It has sharpened my sensory perceptions. Certainly, I am deeply attuned to the natural world. I also think that my awareness of the natural world and how the earth speaks to us comes from my work on the farm and my upbringing in a rural part of eastern North Carolina. Further, I believe that haiku has helped me nurture a deep appreciation of nature. I also feel that haiku takes one on a spiritual journey. The spiritual journeys that I have taken through haiku have literally changed me.

How have I changed haiku? Perhaps I have changed haiku. It's interesting that you say that about my haiku. However, I will say that I think I've done some things with haiku, especially with *Desert Storm: A Brief History* that I hadn't seen in other haiku collections. The book focuses on individual soldiers and witnesses to the war. My brother, in fact, served there. Many of things that he told me were horrific. I also interviewed my father, who served two tours of duty in Vietnam. Though I've served in the military, I never had the experience of serving in a war. I served in "peace" time. The time that I spent talking with my father, my brother, and other veterans made this book a part of the living history of that war. In choosing to use haiku to narrate these very difficult experiences, I was able to frame the violence—the sounds and the silences of it—as well as the healing we needed to recover from it in a special way. Using haiku as my foundation, I was also able to depict the realities of this particular war for those who did not experience it and for those who needed to heal from the experience.

SSM: I love the textures of that book, the different experiences that you narrate, the things that you would notice walking around in the street or walking into a military compound. I especially liked your focus on women warriors in the book. So, I have to thank you for writing about the women and African Americans who serve in wartime and who, quite often, are erased from history.

LDM: Oh, you're welcome. I wanted to include all those things. I'm glad that you brought that up because certainly women were a part of the first Gulf War as well as the current wars in Iraq and Afghanistan. How can you leave them out and not tell their stories and erase them from the narrative, from the history, and from the canon? What I tried to do with *Desert Storm: A Brief History* was to include the diverse groups of people who served in that war: women, African Americans, and individuals whom the world of historians often neglects.

SSM: Before you picked up your pen to write for the first time, had you ever studied haiku?

LDM: Truly, I had not studied haiku when I first began to write. The fact that I was even considering writing as my vocation, as an African American from the South, and from eastern North Carolina at that time was really quite extraordinary. However, when my sister learned that I was writing haiku, she informed me a teacher that we both had in high school had taught us haiku. I had not even remembered it. So, it's even more remarkable that I have made haiku one of my most cherished art forms as a poet. However, I had studied the usual white poets in my education, Robert Frost and Edgar Allan Poe among others. It was in the early 1980s while I was serving in the military and stationed in what was then West Germany—the Berlin Wall was still in place—while taking a creative-writing class at the University of Maryland Overseas Branch, I had the opportunity to study African American poets. I started with Gwendolyn Brooks then moved to Langston Hughes and never looked back.

SSM: Let's discuss the work that haiku projects that you have brought to fruition. I am especially interested in hearing about your daughter Maiisha, who was a poet in her own right, before her untimely death. What was really meaningful about passing the craft to Maiisha? What do you think would have been her legacy had she had the opportunity to develop her craft?

LDM: Maiisha was doing really well with her poetry, and she was especially doing well with haiku. In fact, she had haiku published in one of the anthologies that the North Carolina Haiku Society published several years ago. It was probably two decades ago. She was published in *Catch the Fire*. I believe that book came out in 1998, and she was excited to write haiku. I remember once we were riding down Barwell Road, this must have been the late eighties, and she recited a haiku to me. Of course, I had to write it down.

SSM: How old was she then?

LDM: She was five years old; she was really young, probably about five or six. Before she died, this must have been in probably 2002 or 2003, we took a family trip to the Bahamas. We often wrote haiku as a family when we traveled. She took my notebook and wrote her haiku in it while we were on the plane. Even now, I often read her haiku, several of which were published, and two of which were published in a special issue of *Obsidian* focused on North Carolina writers. In fact, one of my most famous haiku was composed after my hand literally started to sing while I was touching her coffin. The poem won numerous awards and was published in the *Heron's Nest*:

> hot afternoon
> the squeak of my hands
> on my daughter's coffin

In fact, it's been anthologized. The poem won Valentine's Award for Poem of the Year, and I was awarded Poet of the Year for that one. I actually wrote my way through the grief of her death, and she continues to inspire me, although she died in 2004. I have only recently completed a collection of poems, many of which were written immediately following her transition. It's titled "Dear Maiisha." Several of the poems have already been published in different journals.

SSM: I was so pleased to have the opportunity to include her work in that special issue. Lenard, I know that you are a person who walks around with several journals so that you can write all the time. What do you do with these journals that are chock-full of poems that we have yet to see?

LDM: You know I carry these notebooks around. I write haiku all the time, and I write tanka, another Japanese form of poetry, as well. I enjoy writing that so much that I always keep my notebooks with me. I also always have several ink pens on me. A lot of times, I have more than one journal on me. I don't want to miss any of the haiku moments that might present themselves to me. There are also times when I go to certain events such as a jazz concert from which I am inspired to write. I'm always jotting down notes or trying to write a poem or two in response to what I hear. The same thing happens when I go to an art museum. I'm usually writing responses to the artwork. These moments always inspire me in some way or another. That is why I am always prepared to write. I never want to miss a single moment.

SSM: What's next for you? When will your readers have the opportunity to see what is in your journals?

LDM: What I hope to do is to get out a collection of jazz-related poetry or jazz poetry. I have been working on that for a long time. I listen to jazz every day as I work and look for those moments of inspiration. I have several completed manuscripts including a haiku collection, a tanka collection, and a jazz poetry collection. I've been savoring and saving this work for many years, sometimes for decades. I have also wanted my fiction to compete with poetry. I am compiling a collection of short stories and have also been working on a novella.

SSM: Can we say that you are continually inspired by music, nature, your roots in rural North Carolina, and your muse, Maiisha?

LDM: Absolutely [*he laughs, with his hand on his forehead and his journal at hand*].

SSM: That's a good place for us to stop, at least until the contents of your journals have been revealed?

LDM: Yes, it is. Thank you for giving me the opportunity to discuss my work with you.

An Interview with Lenard D. Moore

John Zheng / 2017

From *Valley Voices: A Literary Review* 17, no. 2 (2017): 40–55. Reprinted by permission of *Valley Voices: A Literary Review.*

John Zheng: You have published five collections of poetry, *Poems of Love & Understanding* by Carlton Press in 1982; *The Open Eye* by the North Carolina Haiku Society Press in 1985 and by the Mountains and Rivers Press in 2015 in a limited thirtieth-anniversary edition; *Forever Home* by Saint Andrews Press in 1992; *Desert Storm: A Brief History* by Los Hombres Press in 1993; and *A Temple Looming* by WordTech Editions in 2008. I'll ask you questions later about your haiku. For now, I'm focusing on your free verse. I guess, your first book—*Poems of Love & Understanding*—might be a chapbook of free verse. How did you start writing it?

Lenard D. Moore: *Poems of Love and Understanding* is a chapbook, which consists of acrostic poems, rhyming poems, lyric poems, and free verse poems. St. Andrews College Press published the second printing of *Forever Home* with a new front cover in 1996. You are right in that St. Andrews Press published the first edition in 1992. Please note that the word College is in the publisher's name for the second printing of *Forever Home.* In *Forever Home,* my poem "Onslow County, North Carolina," on page 47, is dedicated to Bashō; it is a six-line poem. The book has three sections. Guy Davenport wrote an introduction for *Forever Home.* Fred Chappell wrote an afterword for *Forever Home.* The poems are about family, farming, and ancestors. My love of language led me to writing. For example, I read books on the long bus ride to elementary school. My grandfather told my brothers, sisters, and me stories. His storytelling was very interesting and captivating. In school, we had to memorize poems and recite them in class. In seventh grade, I wrote a play, which some of my classmates and I staged. In fact, we acted in the play during class. In tenth grade, I wrote short stories for class. At that same time, I was writing poetry, which rhymed. When I was a soldier in the US Army, I began writing poetry every day.

JZ: Oh, you nurtured your creativity at such a young age. Was your poetry mainly about military life when you were a soldier? Also, does your poem "Onslow County, North Carolina," dedicated to Bashō, reflect any haiku elements? Since it's a six-line poem, can you show it to us here?

LDM: No, my poetry was not mainly about my military experience. Yes, there is the influence of haiku in my poem "Onslow County, North Carolina" from my poetry book, *Forever Home*. Here is the poem:

> "Onslow County, North Carolina"
> —*for Bashō*

In windless moonlight
black spider weaving its web,
a poised firefly blinks
among the fallen plum tree,
and, in the garden,
cricket song rises and falls.

Hopefully, the above poem is lyrical and full of good details and strong verbs. Like a haiku, the poem is about what is happening now and employs vivid imagery. Perhaps you are interested in knowing that I also write ars poetica, blank verse, blues poems, cobla, dramatic monologues, ekphrastic poetry, elegies, epithalamiums, georgics, ghazals, haibun, idyll, kwansabas, lyric poems, object poems, pantoums, prose poems, renga, renku, sentence poems, sequences, sestinas, syllabics, tanka, triolets, epistles or letter poems, villanelles, and jazz poems.

JZ: It's interesting that your poem "Onslow County, North Carolina" has a five-seven-five-seven-five-seven pattern. It's also interesting to know that you write all these forms of poems. I remember *Valley Voices* published your blues and jazz poems. Is your ekphrastic poetry based on art or photography?

LDM: I hope the reader will be able to see a connection to haiku and maybe tanka when reading my poem "Onslow County, North Carolina." To that end, the musical elements which I have employed in the poem are important to the poem's movement and progression. All of the poems in *A Temple Looming* are based on photographs. In fact, they were mostly black-and-white photographs from about one hundred years ago.

JZ: What was your commitment at some point when you decided to become a poet?

LDM: When I became a poet, my commitment was to write daily or as often as possible. I also wanted to ensure that I employed much figurative language. However, music or rhythm was one of the most important literary elements for me, including alliteration, assonance, consonance, euphony, repetition, and rhyme. Then, too, I somehow wrote with imagery and symbolism in mind. I wanted to document daily life, the natural world, historical events, ancestral stories, and the cultural arts.

JZ: As for the music and rhythm in your poetry, is there any influence from the African American church? And how does it influence your writing?

LDM: Yes, I am sure that there is some kind of influence of the African American church on my writing. Of course, I am aware of the cadence of the preacher's sermons and the rhythm of the gospel choir. When growing up, I attended church with my family on a frequent basis. In fact, I have written about church experiences regarding listening to gospel music and sermons. When I was in my twenties, I served as an usher at church. One of my great-aunts played the piano at church; she also had a piano at her house. In short, I listened to the music often, including on vinyl LPs and on the radio.

JZ: So, is it fair to say that growing up African American has been an influence on your poetry? Can you use a poem of yours to elaborate on this influence?

LDM: I think my poem "A Circle of Hands" shows the influence of growing up African American, especially because of the bond of family and the importance of music:

"A Circle of Hands"
—*for Terrance Hayes and Yona Harvey*

After midnight,
the sky pulls itself down
to drought-burned slopes.

I have forgotten my feet ache.
Thrilled with the full house,
the harmonica whining blues

in the far corner:
a couple hugged up in an armchair;
husband blowing blue

notes back on himself.
The wife reads *Mosquito & Ant*,
brown fingers peeling pages.

I am inside the card game,
the harmonica, the bent-back book,
but do not know how I got here.

I do not know how to leave.
Cards slap the table,
breath makes the harmonica speak

of the dreadlocked woman,
of the spine-snapped book,
of the rain that does not fall.

JZ: The creative process would be of interest to readers. Can you talk a bit about how you create a poem?

LDM: When writing a poem, I start with an image, place, or event, such as a historical event or a cultural event. In fact, I often write while listening to jazz. The jazz might be on satellite, car radio, CD player, online, concert, etcetera. My grandfather was a great storyteller. In short, he has also inspired me to write poetry. There are times when I visit an art museum or a history museum where I write poetry about paintings, photographs, or artifacts. In addition, I explore memory, family, quilts, and the natural world. Then I try to employ fresh metaphors, good similes, and other literary elements in my poetry writing. Yet it is very important for me to employ music in my poetry. Moreover, I try to make parallels and connections, turn phrases, and take leaps with my poetry writing. I hope to create meanings that matter in my poetry. At times, the poetic form, which I might employ, guides me along the way with my poetry writing. Thus, I really like a sense of discovery whenever I write poetry. All the while, I employ the five senses in my poetry writing and hope that my poetry is memorable.

JZ: Your grandfather was a great storyteller and inspired you to write poetry. So, do you tend to use the Black dialect often or the so-called standard English when you write poetry? You also like to write while listening to jazz. Does this help your poetic lines flow with a jazz rhythm?

LDM: It depends upon what kind of poem I might write about whether I employ standard English or the Black dialect. For example, I employ Black dialect when I write a blues poem. At times, I might employ Black dialect when I incorporate dialogue, especially if there is a particular kind of storytelling in my poem. For the most part, I employ standard English when I write poetry. Yes, I think listening to jazz helps to enhance the music in my poetry writing. However, many times I write in silence, especially while enjoying the natural world and viewing a painting or photograph. There are times when I catch a rhythm while writing poetry. In short, I use different approaches to writing poetry.

JZ: Then, can we say there is a "twoness" or dichotomy in your poetry writing? Or can we say you use Black dialect to write poetry about the Black experience and standard English to write poetry about the experience not specifically race related? Can you share with us a story about writing about these experiences?

LDM: No, I use standard English to write most of my poetry. I seldom use Black dialect to write poetry, except when writing blues poetry. However, I did use Black dialect in some of my poetry writing in the early 1980s. I think I might have used Black dialect a few other times, though I prefer using standard English to write poetry. So, I do not think I have a story about writing about using Black dialect or standard English. I hope to write the best poem that I can possibly write. In short, I try to employ music in my poetry. Yet, I strive for clarity and multiple meanings in my poetry.

JZ: So, music has played an important part in your writing. Poetry is an art of form, and it helps bridge the poet and the reader. You said earlier that the poetic form you employed guided you with your poetry writing. How did you play with a form, be it in meter or in free verse?

LDM: When I write poetry using poetic forms, those poetic forms take my poetry writing into new turns and new territory. For example, I do not know where the poem will lead me. I simply pay close attention and follow the poem wherever it goes. In short, there is a sense of discovery for me. I am not saying that when writing free verse, I know where the poem might take me because I do not. However, writing poetry in poetic forms seems to be more challenging. One of my sestinas has been reprinted a number of times. One of my villanelles has been published in a major anthology. There are also many other poetic forms, which I employ when writing.

JZ: Poetry is an art of the spoken word, but nowadays more and more readers treat poetry as printed words and read it silently. How do you reach your audience as a facilitator of poetry in North Carolina?

LDM: I try to reach my audience by presenting a lively reading. To that end, I strive for music in my poetry. I also strive for vivid imagery in my poetry. I think collaborations are very important, too. I have collaborated with dancers, musicians, painters, photographers, and quilters. My poetry has been exhibited with quilts, paintings, photographs, and sheet music in galleries, museums, and cultural arts centers. My poetry has also been featured with slides. Many times, I have performed my poetry with jazz bands and solo jazz musicians. Several times, I have engaged my audiences by asking them to participate in my poetry readings with a call and response or to repeat the refrain. There have been times when I sang my poems in the company of musicians. When I perform with musicians, I usually write poems or lyrics for the events. In 2012, I performed with the University of Mount Olive's Symphony. I wrote the poems for that performance, too. Those are some of the ways that I have engaged my audiences with my poetry readings and performances.

JZ: It's fascinating that you have performed your poetry with musicians and exhibited it with other art forms. Can you talk specifically about your poetry performance with the jazz band that took place at the University of North Carolina at Chapel Hill in spring 2017? How was your collaboration with the band? Did you perform jazz poems? And how did the audiences respond to your performance?

LDM: Yes, I performed my jazz poetry with the University of Mount Olive Jazz Band in the "Music on the Front Porch Series" at the Center for the Study of the American South at the University of North Carolina at Chapel Hill. I sat in on the jazz band's practices and wrote poetry to the rhythm of each tune. It usually took only one or two takes for me to finish writing a poem for each tune. When I felt that I had a poem or lyrics that could work in collaboration with the jazz band, then we performed together. Dr. William Ford directed the University of Mount Olive Jazz Band and arranged the order of the songs/poems. I announced certain instruments in my poems and/or incorporated the types of instruments. I think it worked well because the jazz band and I were having fun performing. Then, too, the music and poems worked well together. It seems that the audience was very engaged. They sang, clapped, and smiled. Of course, I enjoy writing jazz poetry. I collaborated with the University of Mount Olive Jazz in 2015 as well as this spring (2017). I wrote the poetry/lyrics for that performance, too.

JZ: We read to learn from the perspectives of others about the world. Can you talk about writing what you see and what you know by using imagery in your poetry?

LDM: Yes, I certainly employ imagery in my poetry because I believe it helps readers to connect better with poetry. To that end, I think readers would be able to see and hear what the poet sees and hears within the captured moment. Hopefully, more meanings will surface for my readers. However, craft is definitely pertinent for me. For example, my books *A Temple Looming*, *Forever Home*, and *The Open Eye* rely heavily on imagery.

JZ: I'd like to go back to the discussion of form and know more about your writing process. Form comes out of a significant moment, historical, cultural, or personal. Written in language, the form shows the poet's personal preference and his or her attempt to deal with the moment. How do you tie the content to the form?

LDM: When writing poetry in form, the content drives it from start to finish. For example, when writing haiku, the moment and natural world inspire me. When writing about love or relationships, tanka works well as the form, because it is lyrical and lends itself to containing the juxtaposition. The sonnet form also works well for the subject of love because of the rhythm, rhyme, turn, and resolution. A blues poem relies heavily on form with its rhythm, rhyme, repetition, and tone. A jazz poem relies on improvisation, phrasing, imagery, and sound. However, I have written several poems in syllabics. To that end, I know what the structure of the poem will be though not where it might end. Once I begin writing a poem, the figurative language has a way of driving the poem. In short, I hope to write the best poem that I possibly can.

JZ: Now I want to ask you to talk about your haiku writing.

LDM: When I'm not teaching, I spend much of my time writing haiku. When January of 2018 arrives, it will be thirty-six years that I have been writing haiku. I find that haiku writing helps my longer forms of poetry writing because of the concise language, precision of details, and juxtaposition of unlike images. I keep one or two journals and ink pens with me so that I can capture the haiku moment whenever it appears. Thus, there is the influence of haiku throughout my poetry book, *Forever Home* (St. Andrews Press, 1992). Moreover, I have written several haiku sequences. I have also collaborated with other poets to write renga and renku. In addition, I have read and performed my haiku with jazz bands and solo jazz musicians, including bassists. For me, haiku is a way of life. I live haiku without reserve.

JZ: So, you live a haiku life. Does the influence of haiku throughout *Forever Home* also indicate an interdependence or interaction between your haiku and your longer forms of poetry writing, such as free verse? What I mean is that the influence is a two-way process.

LDM: No, I don't think my haiku and free verse are interdependent. However, there are a few of the poems in which I employ some techniques of haiku writing in *Forever Home*. In fact, there is a poem dedicated to Bashō in the book. There also is an ars poetica as well as other lyric poems. Then, too, there are narrative poems in *Forever Home*. I think I'll leave the analysis of *Forever Home* to my readers, literary scholars, and literary critics. I hope the book appeals to my readers' emotions. Let's see what happens with the persona's voice in *Forever Home*.

JZ: As the executive chairman of the North Carolina Haiku Society, what have you been doing to promote haiku or inspire young haiku poets?

LDM: I have been assisting with the programming for the North Carolina Haiku Society's Annual Haiku Holiday Conference. Since 1983, I have attended each one of the North Carolina Haiku Society's Annual Haiku Holiday Conferences. I also teach the haiku workshop at the haiku holiday conferences. Sometimes I invite other poets to teach or coteach a workshop or give a presentation on haiku. Dave Russo also helps with coordinating the haiku holiday conference. After the North Carolina Haiku Society founder Rebecca Ball Rust moved away, I coordinated the haiku holiday conferences alone. Several years ago, I was the membership coordinator and treasurer. The North Carolina Haiku Society does not charge dues any longer, so there is no longer a treasurer. Members sign up to receive the online newsletter, which Dave Russo sends out from time to time. He also organizes ginkos and a few workshops for members. I usually attend all the ginkos and workshops. Oftentimes I write several haiku on the ginkos. I have invited younger poets to give presentations at the North Carolina Haiku Society's Annual Haiku Holiday Conference. In addition, I mentor several poets. To that end, I help them with their haiku study and practice.

JZ: Red Moon Press published your *Gathering at the Crossroads* in 2003. I am curious about your photo-poetic collaboration with Eugene B. Redmond and wonder whether your haiku are ekphrastic based on his photographs. Can you talk about it?

LDM: For the chapbook *Gathering at the Crossroads*, I wrote the haiku and then asked Eugene B. Redmond to send some of his photographs of the Million Man March for the project. The Red Moon Press publisher selected the photographs from Eugene B. Redmond's photographs and then paired up the poems and photography. The photography is great. I hope the poems resonate. I like the collaboration.

JZ: I was reading Jane Hirshfield's *Ten Windows: How Great Poems Transform the World*, in which Bashō advises that "unless things are seen with fresh eyes, nothing's worth writing down." How do you catch things with fresh eyes for your haiku writing?

LDM: I try to stay attuned to the natural world with my eyes wide open and my ears turned to what's happening. For me, my haiku writing embodies a oneness with nature. I hope I am able to freeze such special moments in time. Jane Hirshfield certainly is an outstanding poet. I have read some of her earlier poetry. I look forward to reading her book *Ten Windows: How Great Poems Transform the World.* I want to write poems that are memorable.

JZ: Everydayness is important in poetry writing. How do you deal with this theme in your haiku or other types of poetry?

LDM: Yes, everydayness is very important to my poetry because I often write about observation. Then, too, I write from experience and memory. All three of them are key to my writing. Within my writing, oftentimes memory and history intersect. Yet I strive for clarity. Moreover, it is my hope that my poetry is accessible to my readers. Moreover, I try to reveal identity in my poetry. In short, this is my way of capturing the everydayness within my poetry.

JZ: How do you reveal or explore identity, and how important is identity in relation to history, race, language, and geography in your poetry?

LDM: There are a number of ways I explore identity in my poetry. For example, I employ allusions and cultural references in my poetry. I also think voice, language, and geography help to explore identity in my poetry. I believe that language and geography help to shape my idea of what might be possible in poetry. There are times when race enters a poem, but I do not think I have it in mind when writing poetry. Like any other poet, I just want to write the best poem that I possibly can. To that end, I wonder why there might be labels for poets of color. Maybe race in poetry helps to create labels. I am an American poet. It is obvious that I am African American. Yet, there are certain historical events that poets of color might experience. When reading some of my poetry, I believe the identity reveals itself. For example, in my poem "Praisesong: From Son to Mother" in *Forever Home*, the opening line reads as: "Mother, I listen hard to hear you speak," and later, lines 27 and 28 read as "your oldest manchild / praying long this night." In the first line, the reader knows that an offspring speaks, and later in the poem, the gender is revealed. So, I believe these are some of the ways that I reveal and/or explore identity in my poetry. For me, the most important thing is craft. Thus, I work hard on my craft. Like a bucket holding water, I want the form to contain the content so that the poem exists in the best possible light. In short, that is the way I imagine poetic form to work. Within that body of language, identity surfaces. Then, too, I have employed the word *black* in some of my poetry. There are times when I employ contrasts. I hope I have given some insight into my poetry, though I prefer for the reader to find his or her own meanings in my poetry. Thank you very much for such another thought-provoking question.

JZ: I agree that poets should not be labeled by color or race, though oftentimes poetry we write may reflects that, as in your poem "Praisesong: From Son to Mother." It would be good to share it with readers:

Mother, I listen hard to hear you speak
how grandfather plowed
behind the largest mule
in dusty sunlight
as nearby elms gave way to wind.
I think of you: how
you picked purple collards
from the backyard garden,
got hot-meat fresh from great-grandma.
This was routine.
At dusk, with father home from teaching mechanics,
you set the redwood table.
We ate by candles.
Nobody spoke, the only sound
the noise of spoons and forks
scraping tin plates.
You guided me through chores:
cooking for younger brothers and sisters
who played daylong on mull-thinned woods;
keeping the large blue house spotless.
Beyond that, you were an artist,
drawing, painting in private hours.
You never knew I saw.
The truth is, I searched out your art
when you were away.
How your love grows into me
your oldest manchild
praying long this night
that we could pass this praisesong on
to those who ache
to know.

Your poem reminds me of Langston Hughes's "Mother to Son," which is a mother's exhortation to her son to follow her steps with courage and perseverance. In both Hughes's poem and yours, the mother figure serves as an example of motivation to their man-children, affirming racial dignity and pride. I think identity or race is not a topic a poet can avoid in their writing, though I agree (allow me to repeat) with you that a poet should not be labeled with race. As a haiku practitioner, can you talk especially about Sonia Sanchez's haiku that shows her identity and characteristic?

LDM: I think Sonia Sanchez creates identity in her haiku with the language, cultural references, and allusions. She also employs references to blues and has a bluesy rhythm and jazzy rhythm in her haiku. She breaks new ground with her haiku, especially musically. In addition, she honors ancestors in her haiku, including her brother. I suggest reading her book *Does Your House Have Lions*? In addition, she works with variations of the haiku with her poetic form sonku. I am honored to know that you have compared my poem, "Praisesong: From Son to Mother" to Langston Hughes's poem "Mother to Son." In fact, I have read and taught Hughes's poetry in my creative-writing classes, African American literature classes, and advanced poetry-writing classes for several years. When I taught my literary forms class, I taught Hughes's poetry in it, too, because I introduced my students to blues poetry. When teaching blues poetry, I have also taught Raymond Patterson's poetry, Sterling Brown's poetry, Sterling Plumpp's poetry, and Sonia Sanchez.

JZ: You mentioned your teaching. Poetry provides a chance for a reader to experience, ponder, or entertain what a poet has presented. How does your teaching make this experience educational and entertaining, especially for a student unaccustomed to poetry reading or writing?

LDM: I think my teaching helps to make poetry educational and entertaining because of the experience that I bring into the classroom. I also think my awareness of history and cultural references help to make the experience educational and entertaining. At least, I hope it works that way for my students. My students usually ask me to read my own poetry, too. Moreover, I strive to present insightful explications of poetry that I teach. In addition, I show video clips of poets reading their poetry and performing with jazz bands. In fact, I employ different teaching modes in the classroom, such as lectures, videos, music, group work, and presentations. Earlier this afternoon, a student informed me that she enjoyed my world literature class last semester. When I teach my creative-writing classes, I show my students how to create a portfolio and present readings. To that end, they turn in creative-writing portfolios and present an end-of-the-semester poetry and fiction reading. There are times when I invite poets to engage in dialogue with my students by way of e-mail. I take my students to the campus library where they sign onto the computers and ask questions on email in regard to a poet's work, especially when I teach the poet's book in the course. So, the poet answers my students' questions about his or her poetry. Moreover, I require them to submit their literary works to literary journals and magazines. In short, I believe in them having the experience of poets. Thus, I hope to prepare my students for the life of a writer or poet.

JZ: Can we go back to talk a little about haiku? I enjoyed reading David Lanoue's review of your *Gathering at the Crossroads*. He says you invite the reader into a world in which so much is not described nor explained. Can you use a haiku of yours to explain how the reader can fill the "unspoken gaps" to gain what is not described?

LDM: Yes, we can go back to talk about haiku. I really like reading, studying, and writing haiku. I also like experimenting with the haiku form. Several years ago, I told a poet that I employ three of the five senses in my haiku and that many poets employ only two of the senses in their haiku. What I could not believe is that I later read an article the other poet wrote about what I had said. Perhaps, it is not best to tell others about one's writing process until he or she writes and publishes it himself or herself.

Let's get to the haiku that you have requested. I do not think that the poet should employ everything in his or her haiku. The poet should not underestimate the reader. I believe the reader can participate in the experience of the haiku and bring his or her own experience into the reading of the haiku. Here is one of my haiku from *The Open Eye*:

a black woman
breastfeeding her infant—
the autumn moon

This haiku previously appeared on page 46, in the October 6, 1985, issue of *Sunday Mainichi Weekly Magazine* in Tokyo, Japan.

JZ: Can you explain your employment of three of the five senses in your haiku?

LDM: Yes, my haiku "hot afternoon" is an example of how I employed three of the five senses into my haiku. The first line, "hot afternoon," employs tactile imagery. The second line, "the squeak of my hands," employs auditory imagery. The third line or last line, "on my daughter's coffin," employs visual imagery. This haiku was originally published in the *Heron's Nest* and has since been reprinted several times.

JZ: Bill Ferris says in his article "A Sense of Place" that within us there is a "sense of place" about where we are born and grow up that defines and shapes us. In your haiku practice, how does your sense of place, history, or culture shape your creative thinking and writing about the world?

LDM: Bill Ferris is a great scholar and photographer. He definitely captures a sense of place in his work. I have a few of his books, including his most recent book that features his photography. I think my haiku practice helps to shape my creative thinking and writing about the natural world. When writing haiku, one must always be aware of his or her surroundings. Thus, I document the natural world with my haiku. I record significant events, cultural events, and place often in my haiku practice. In short, I am attuned to the natural world. Earlier today [October 2, 2017] I sent some of my longer poems to you, including several in fixed forms. I hope those poems show my range. I have employed anaphora in my poem "Azalea, Azalea" toward the closure. I hope it is evident that I employ as much figurative language as possible in my poetry. I want to create texture in my poetry. Perhaps the idea of creating texture in my poetry causes me to employ three of the five senses in my haiku writing.

JZ: Nowadays, haiku poets have written too many haiku about nature. This is fine, but it seems that senryu, which usually has an ironic tone and a focus on human nature, can be more appealing to readers, especially those unfamiliar with haiku. Which genre appeals more to you, haiku or senryu?

LDM: This past summer I edited a forthcoming book titled *One Window's Light*. The collection does not just include haiku about nature; it includes haiku about family, historical events, etcetera. *One Window's Light* is a collection of haiku by five members of the Carolina African American Writers' Collective. So, to answer your question, I must say that haiku appeals to me more than senryu.

JZ: You have written some one-line haiku, which is termed monoku by Jim Kacian. Since most haiku are written in three lines in English, can you talk about how you decide a one-liner may be more effective than a three-liner?

LDM: When I started writing haiku in 1982, I do not think the term *monoku* had been coined. Thus, I did not have it in mind when I wrote my one-line haiku. I wrote the way I felt the subject needed to be documented. My early one-line haiku hopefully captured the rhythm of the experience. In fact, my one-line haiku can be read in one breath.

JZ: What's your current writing project?

LDM: One of my writing projects, which I finished the poems earlier this year, is a collaboration with one of my former students whom I taught twenty years ago at North Carolina State University. She is an excellent photographer and the department chair at a college. She did the photography for the project. I wrote longer poems about the photos. When I say longer poems, I mean poems that are longer than haiku. She has the vision for an exhibit and a book.

Now I plan to work on a writing project that will be a collaboration with my brother-in-law, who is a doctor and a photographer. He has taken great photos of the natural world. I hope to write longer poems about them. Both of us are excited about the project. Then, too, I look forward to the publication of my next poetry collection, *The Geography of Jazz*.

Mentoring a New Generation of African American Haiku Writers: Interview with Lenard D. Moore

Crystal Simone Smith / 2020

From *African American Review* 56, no. 1 (2023): 1–8. Reprinted by permission.

Part 1

Crystal Simone Smith: As one of the leading haiku poets in the United States, your individual accomplishments include five poetry collections, an extensive list of major awards, including three Haiku Museum of Tokyo Awards, and being the first African American elected as president of the Haiku Society of America. In addition, you have collaborated often through the years with fellow writers partnering in projects and publishing anthologies. I'll begin with a three-part question. First, do you feel a sense of mastery of the haiku form? Please expound.

Lenard D. Moore: First, let me say that I have eight poetry collections. I have also edited and/or coedited eight anthologies. In addition, there is a collaborative project titled the Satire Project, which includes a DVD titled *The Satire Project*. There is a chapbook titled *The Satire Project*, which includes Professor Larry Lean's visual art/paintings, my poetry inspired by Professor Lean's visual art/paintings, and Dr. William Goss's sheet music from my poems. I am the vocals on the DVD. Professor Lean created and designed the DVD. Dr. Goss recorded my reading, performing, and singing my poems during spring break in 2016.

During the summer of 2020, I was appointed as honorary curator of the American Haiku Archives at California State Library in Sacramento. You can visit the link to learn more about the honorary curator of the American Haiku Archives appointment. Yes, I have collaborated with several others:

poets, painters, photographers, dancers, musicians, etcetera. Most notably, I have collaborated with the renowned Black arts movement poet Eugene B. Redmond on the chapbook *Gathering at the Crossroads*. The chapbook includes my haiku and Professor Redmond's photography of the Million Man March. I feel like I really know the haiku because I have been reading, studying, and writing haiku for so long now. In January 2021, it will make thirty-nine years that I have been writing haiku. Of course, I have been experimenting with the haiku form for decades. To that end, I have been writing bluesku and jazzku as I called them in an interview that Dr. Doris Lucas Laryea conducted about twenty-five years ago. The interview was published in *Obsidian* about twenty-four years ago. So, it is well documented. In addition, I have been writing gospelku or gospel haiku for a very long time, too. Then, too, I have been writing Afrofuturistic haiku. More than two decades ago, I told someone that I had been writing haiku with three of the sensory perceptions rather than two of them as I saw in many haiku that I studied long ago.

Consequently, I saw somewhere that the person whom I told what I was doing with haiku then wrote an article about what I was longing for, but I wrote the article as his own. In short, I have learned not to discuss what projects I might engage in. Similarly, I have noticed over the years that when I include titles of projects that I am working on at the time in my bios, somehow others might have a book with that title or those titles. If I do not answer anything fully, I think you would understand. However, I am trying to answer your questions completely for this interview. Haiku is a way of life for me. I hope I have made haiku my own mode of expression while documenting the phenomenon. I am grateful to you for wanting to interview me.

CSS: Second, early African American haiku poets like Etheridge Knight, Robert Hayden, and Richard Wright were denied equal visibility in the American haiku movement. To date, you have published more haiku than any African American. In what ways do you feel connected to those writers and their legacies and what role(s) have you taken as a mentor for a new generation of African American haiku poets?

LDM: Louis G. Alexander wrote haiku during the Harlem Renaissance. I believe he is the Father of African American haiku. I also believe we owe much gratitude to Richard Wright for bringing greater awareness to African American haiku. Sonia Sanchez has sparked much interest in African American haiku. Robert Hayden wrote memorable haiku. Etheridge Knight wrote outstanding haiku. Kalamu ya Salaam deserves more attention for writing haiku. Yes, I have been blessed to have my haiku published in many publications throughout this country and many other countries and translated into several languages, including Japanese. I feel very connected to the earlier African American haiku poets, especially Richard Wright. I stand on my elders' shoulders. I also owe much praise to my ancestors. I definitely owe much kudos to all the Japanese haiku, which was translated into English. To that end, I began writing traditional haiku, but I mostly write contemporary haiku nowadays.

I have experimented with one-word haiku, three-word haiku, one-line haiku, and four-word haiku. My one-word haiku was dedicated to Elizabeth Searle Lamb and published in the haiku magazine titled *Wind Chimes*, which was published in Maryland in the 1980s. I experimented with the structure of a book-length haiku sequence for my book *Desert Storm: A Brief History*. I wanted to employ narrative elements and other literary elements within that book. In short, I hope I have contributed to the American haiku movement and the African American haiku movement. I say African American haiku movement because I have taught several African American haiku poets to write haiku for more than three decades. Many of them are publishing haiku on a regular basis. I compiled and edited a collection of African American haiku a quarter of a century ago, but I could not get it published because publishers, at that time, did not think enough African Americans wrote haiku. In short, I have been involved with ecopoetic writing for about four decades, but it was not called that so long ago. Let me say that I have also taught my students how to write haiku for decades. I have also submitted their poetry to magazines and have gotten some of them published. When I taught composition, I had an assignment in which my students brought hometown newspapers to class to discuss articles in them. Then I taught them how to write letters to the editor in response to the articles. I also taught them how to write cover letters and how to prepare self-addressed stamped envelopes (SASE). Then I took their prepared submissions to the post office. Many of them got published in their hometown newspapers.

My point is that I taught students from many different backgrounds, races, and cultures. I have also mentored my students and older adult poets and writers. I learn from my students, too. For me, learning works both ways, from the teacher and the student/s. Like my prose teaching, I have tried to be as engaging with my haiku. I hope my answer is not too long because I feel connected to my students and others whom I have taught and/or mentored. Yet, I am constantly striving to do something new with my haiku.

CSS: Lastly, how has collaborative writing, particularly with other Black haiku poets, further enriched or enhanced your haiku journey? Of your many collaborations, I would like to explore two publications. *Gathering at the Crossroads* is a pairing of Eugene Redmond's photography with your haiku sequence memorializing the Million Man March in 1995. *One Window's Light* is a ground-breaking, coauthored collection of haiku you compiled and edited in 2018.

LDM: The collaborative projects have enabled me to see the published books, exhibitions, and recordings in a new light. The collaborations are the only ways that those projects would have been able to come to fruition. They open my imagination further. They have also enabled me to come up with hopefully compelling titles for the projects. In fact, my collaborative haiku projects with Black poets garnered a number of firsts, including the structure of the books and the kinds of museum collaborations, etcetera. If you are collaborating with extraordinary writers and/or artists, it somehow propels you to the next level. That is the way I feel about the chapbook and the anthology. I did not want to structure the anthology by the four seasons like so many other haiku books. I employed different themes to link the haiku as if they were in conversation. I always believe in doing something new. There are countless books published each year. So how would one get his or her book to stand out and hopefully get reviewed and garner a wider readership? Would I want to write the book?

CSS: The sequence in *Gathering at the Crossroads* spans a day from dawn until dusk chronicling a political event organized to empower millions of Black men. As attendees, the response is two part—that of Redmond's photographic lens and your composed haiku. Can you describe the importance of documenting the day in dual ways and the process of your collaboration?

LDM: I think it is important to document such political events with poetry and photography because they both lend themselves to different ways of seeing things. One might say photography gives you what is there, but I think it provides more, especially when considering color, shadows, light, contrast, rhythm, perspective, shapes, figures or objects, the natural world, background, and so forth. One might also say that poetry triggers one to find the gaps, but it incorporates several literary elements. For example, I strive to employ good details, vivid imagery, contrast, juxtaposition, rhythm, kigo, two parts (cutting word), and music in my haiku. Yet, collaboration might lead me to shift my approach to writing, compiling, and editing.

CSS: The sequence embodies the essential haiku element of nature. The reader emerges on a clear autumn day, and the perceived colors of autumn juxtaposed with a million Black faces create a metaphorical dim and vivid tension in each haiku that renders its own harmony. This is present in the following haiku:

> on the stage
> a line of brothers locks arms
> autumn sunshine

Of the individual haiku in the sequence, which moment do you feel closest to and why?

LDM: I think I feel closest to my following haiku from the sequence:

> sun plaza:
> one million shadows darken
> foot by foot

I like the above haiku best from the sequence because I feel that it opens up a number of possibilities. There also is the implied sound or rhythm of all the feet. Additionally, there is such a large number of men participating in the march. I think the second line embodies mystery and something readying to happen. Then, too, the "shadows" contrast with all the light from the "sun" in the "plaza" in the poem. Moreover, there is the silence blending with the feet rhythm. Somehow, it seems that the poem expands beyond its frame or form. Furthermore, the poem suggests men without saying it. If the sequence was not part of the chapbook, I think the above poem resonates alone.

Part 2

CSS: In *One Window's Light*, you intertwine poems by five African American haiku poets, including yours and poets newer to the form. Can you elaborate on the process of arranging poems written by poets who share cultural connections yet possess distinctive voices and life experiences?

LDM: I read and reread all of the poems. I saw certain themes emerging. I also noticed the various predominant subjects. Additionally, I noticed that there were similarities in topics. Moreover, I decided to arrange the poems in ways that I had not seen in any haiku books. I have been reading haiku books for decades from the United States and several other countries. To that end, I had an idea as to what had never been done in haiku books. Furthermore, I think I knew what made an exceptionally good haiku. Thus, I think I would work toward that end. When compiling and editing, I considered linking the poems and somehow shifting from time to time as if I were leading a renku session because I have participated in several renku sessions in the United States, Canada, and Japan. Rather than list all of the subject headings here, I hope readers will consult our anthology, *One Window's Light*.

CSS: Considered by some critics as "groundbreaking," in what ways does this collection depart from the traditional practices and expectations of other collaborative haiku collections or anthologies?

LDM: I think the collection is unique because it includes the social ills and political issues as well as the natural world and family. The poems within *One Window's Light* also are in conversation with one another. In other words, the collection does not work like something jumbled. *One Window's Light* works as a collective voice. One poet's poetry needs the next poet's poetry and so forth for the collective to speak the way that I had envisioned. It is also the first published anthology of African American haiku. I say published because I have another manuscript that I compiled and edited decades ago. However, I like how Teresa's quilt works on the cover of the anthology. I have provided the photography for the cover. I also greatly appreciate Teresa's essay about her process for making the quilt as the bookend for the collection. And yet, the title of the collection comes from the first line of one of Teresa's haiku. I hope *One Window's Light* will secure a place within the American and African American canon.

CSS: The haiku are placed into thirteen topic sections like "loss" or "teachings." What is the significance of this organization, and how does it inform the collection or guide the reader?

LDM: I hope the thirteen topic sections will reveal that African Americans write about a wide range of topics and that we infuse the African American experience into the collection. Of course, the African American experience is part of the American experience. How can one truly know haiku without knowing the full range of topics? Maybe my introduction to the collection could answer your question in greater detail. I also hope the thirteen topics will reveal that African Americans have other concerns besides sports and entertainment. We are not monolithic. Lastly, I hope that *One Window's Light* will become a model for other collections.

CSS: Some of the haiku are responses to other art forms like the following by L. Teresa Church:

> statue of a black man
> laden with snow
> distant bells

Church's quilted piece "Pain Glass Window at Mother Emmanuel, Charleston, SC" also appears on the cover, and you are an established author of jazz haiku. In what other ways have you collaborated with other artists and art forms? Is there a most memorable collaboration?

LDM: I know you are asking about other artists, but some of the jazz musicians and bands are among my most memorable collaborations. There have been some collaborations that worked well with timing and with us being in sync and inflow or conversation with one another. Yet, I need to mention the very first time that I read/performed my poetry with a band. It was in October 1999 when I attended Adagio's gig at the Durham Armory. The band consisted of Frankie McInnis on keyboards, Sam Peterkin on bass, Arthur "Ace" Everett on drums, and William "Gino" Faison on saxophone. My friend Frankie called me up from the audience to perform my poetry with them. There were so many people in the audience. However, I was able to catch Adagio's rhythm and blend my vocals. I enjoyed the performance. After that time, I have performed all over the country with jazz musicians and bands. I have also written poems and lyrics while rehearsing with jazz bands. Then we performed together. I like that musical experience very much. I have also had memorable collaborations with visual artists.

CSS: As notable in your earlier collection *The Open Eye*, the haiku in *One Window's Light* also embodies a profound sense of place, southern and rural, and a return to the motherland of Africa in Sheila Smith McKoy's haiku. As such, Black life and Black experience are illuminated through haiku. One could argue this is largely due to your haiku approach and guidance. How many African American haiku poets have you mentored, and can you briefly discuss some of the success stories? What teachings or personal influence do you see visible in their writing?

LDM: There are many poets whom I have mentored. When I was haiku editor of the online magazine *Simply Haiku*, I actually made comments/suggestions on the poets' haiku and asked them to resubmit their revised poems to me. Once I felt that the poems resonated, then I accepted them for publication. I also invited some African American poets as well as others to submit haiku to me. When I edited haiku anthologies, again I made editorial comments/suggestions on some of the haiku. I have a very high standard for myself. So, that is the way I strive to edit haiku collections. I have taught several CAAWC members how to write haiku, haibun, minute poems, kwansabas, other forms, and flash fiction. I continue to mentor several of our fellow CAAWC members. I want to ensure that there are many African Americans who write high-quality haiku so that no one else will think that there are not enough of us writing haiku. I am a graduate Cave Canem Fellow. To that end, I taught a few of my fellow Cave Canem colleagues how to write haiku. I also led renku sessions at Cave Canem whenever I was a fellow there. The renku were published in the back of the Cave Canem anthologies during those years. I was delighted that Sonia Sanchez and Lucille Clifton were among the participants in the renku session one of my three years at Cave Canem. Those renku sessions are very memorable. In addition, I have fond memories of performing my poetry with the University of Mount Olive Jazz Band. Moreover, I have mentored African American haiku poets through the mail and later by email. I like the in-person gatherings at libraries and coffeehouses best, sometimes individually.

CSS: *One Window's Light* is a collaboration of haiku poets from the Carolina African Writers Collective, poets that you workshop with routinely. Are there haiku poets, specifically African American, that you have desired or aspire to collaborate with? If you could draft a proposal, what would be your dream collaboration?

LDM: Of course, you would be on that list of dream collaborators. I would really love to collaborate with Sonia Sanchez, Raquel Bailey, Francis Alexander, and all the *One Window's Light* contributors again. I hope you and I will get the opportunity to collaborate on another haiku project. I would also like to collaborate with Eugene B. Redmond again. Moreover, I would like to collaborate with Evie Shockley.

Part 3

CSS: Sonia Sanchez described her first encounter with haiku in the introduction (*haikuography*) of her 2010 collection *Morning Haiku* as finding herself: "From the moment i found a flowered book high up on a shelf at the 8th Street Bookshop in New York City, a book that announced Japanese haiku; from the moment i opened that book, and read the first haiku, i slid down onto the floor and cried and was changed. i had found me." Can you share "the moment" you encounter haiku and how that moment transitioned into a daily practice that has resulted in a life's journey?

LDM: When I clasped the textbook from my bedroom dresser, a textbook that we used in a creative-writing class that I took at the University of Maryland Overseas Branch in Stuttgart, Germany, I turned pages until I saw haiku, and I was changed at that moment to believe that I could write haiku myself. I had been in bed sick with the flu and lying in my childhood bed. I did not realize that haiku was not so easy to write, but as a beginning haiku poet, I thought I could write them. I did not know any of the guidelines, except for the number of syllables. I began writing traditional haiku with the five-seven-five syllable structure, though I did write several one-line haiku. I kept reading, studying, and writing haiku.

When I started winning a number of haiku contests, then I started studying my own haiku. I would not tell anyone about my process for a long time. I got published in several countries in many publications. To that end, the writing and publishing experience was very rewarding. I began to experiment with the haiku form. I tried to capture jazz. I tried to capture blues. I tried to capture the gospel. If you read early interviews with me, I think it reveals some of what I tried to do through my haiku writing. I also wrote several haiku sequences. I realized that haiku writing enhanced my longer forms of poetry. So, I kept writing haiku. I am still writing haiku.

CSS: You have written thousands of haiku and published them in hundreds of anthologies and literary journals. From a mentor's perspective, what are some best practices you can share for newer haiku poets?

LDM: I think the most important advice is to read and read and read haiku, study them, and write at least one haiku every day for a year. Afterward, assess your haiku and keep studying and writing them. Submit your haiku as often as possible. I also would advise newer haiku poets to create a haiku group and join haiku organizations, such as the Haiku Society of America and the North Carolina Haiku Society. As they sharpen their haiku writing skills, then I would advise newer haiku poets to join international haiku organizations, such as the Haiku International Association (in Japan) and Haiku Canada. There are other haiku organizations in this country, such as Haiku Poets of Northern California.

CSS: What are a few favorite haiku that you have written, and can you share the background stories behind them?

LDM: Here are some of my favorite haiku that I have written:

long after sundown
the sound of ripe plums
plumping the ground

The above haiku reminds me of my childhood homeplace. We had a plum tree that produced yellow plums. My grandmother and other relatives had trees that produced big red plums. When we shook the trees, we heard the plums thudding on the ground. I employed rhythm throughout the poem to create meaning. I also included certain details to capture a sense of place. I wanted the reader to complete the poem with his or her experience. For example, I did not employ the adjective *red* or *yellow* for the plums. I thought that the word *ripe* might add enough to the poem. The vowel *o* in the poem conjures the shape of "plums." There's a near-repetition of "plums" and "plumping" present. Also, notice the rhyme of "sound" and "ground" in the poem. The next one is:

stars
flickering . . .
snow

This poem from my book *The Open Eye* consists of fewer words. I was experimenting with the haiku form. Two of the three words are nouns in the poem. I strongly believe in employing nouns in my poems. The second line consists of one *ing* word or gerund to show continuous motion. I did not employ the word *night* anywhere in the poem because the word *stars* informs the reader that it is nighttime. I did not employ the word *silence* anywhere in the poem, because the word *snow* embodies silence. Also, notice the *s* sounds and the letter *i* twice employed somehow gives the allusion to blinking. Here's another one:

late spring sermon
we honk our horns
for Amen

It was in June 2020, this pandemic year, that I wrote the above poem. We held Sunday service outside. When our outdoor congregation liked how our pastor taught and preached the Word, the car horns honked. Again,

I employed concrete details and musical literary elements and not many words, but hopefully, the poem resonates. The fourth one:

> another gospel song
> streams on the laptop—
> the deepening night

Some mornings, I listen to gospel on the laptop and sing along with it. Nights, I close out the day by listening to gospel again, singing along with it again. The rhythm of this poem seems as if it streams, too. Again, I was experimenting with the haiku form. What is the poem saying? What does the poem mean? How does the poem evoke emotions? The fifth one of my favorite haiku:

> quiet rain
> a Coltrane tune I know
> on the radio

This poem sets the mood for the persona or speaker. The persona identifies with Coltrane and jazz. Is the radio in the house, office, or car? The radio is likely in the car because we usually have more updated technology in our houses and in our offices. Maybe the "quiet rain" alludes to a romantic evening. The poem does not employ the word *soft*, though we notice "quiet rain" falls softly. There are concrete details employed throughout the poem. The short line, long line, short line technique, or structure is employed. The quietness of the rain contrasts with the sound of the "Coltrane tune" in the poem. It slowly builds from quietness to a pleasing sound or enjoyable experience. What does the poem trigger within the reader? What does the poem mean?

What is the poem's tone? Questions for the reader to ponder.

CSS: Today, more Black poets are visible in contemporary haiku journals and in the movement. When you consider the future of Black haiku, how do you envision it in contemporary haiku?

LDM: I envision that the gatekeepers will one day feature sections or spreads or entire issues of Black haiku. My last dream or vision for Black haiku might only happen if we create the venues for ourselves. I say that because there are times when some poets are not invited to submit haiku for certain anthologies. Otherwise, some Black haiku poets might only know about certain anthologies once they are published. Then, too, there are a lot of friendly editors who will invite Black haiku poets to submit their haiku for special anthologies of issues of haiku magazines. The American Haiku movement, however, is slowly becoming more inclusive. I envision a bright future for Black haiku poets. Black haiku poets are being invited to edit or coedit anthologies, judge haiku contests, present workshops, and give readings. Thus, the American Haiku movement becomes richer and richer with each decade. Thank you very much for the interview!

Lenard D. Moore: An Interview

David G. Lanoue / 2021

From *Xavier Review* 41, nos. 1–2 (Spring–Fall 2021): 34–40. Reprinted by permission.

The interview took place via the internet during the first week of January 2021. David G. Lanoue questioned acclaimed African American poet Lenard D. Moore about his writing in general as well as how the current pandemic may have affected it.

David G. Lanoue: 2020 was a hard, strange year with so many changes in lifestyle, in work, in how we relate to one another. How about your poetry? Did anything change about your poetry in 2020? What does it mean to you what you want it to mean to your readers?

Lenard D. Moore: Yes, there were changes to my poetry in 2020, especially with the topics and delivery of readings. All of my readings were by way of Zoom. Maybe I should say I presented Zoom readings. I taught poetry workshops on Zoom. Zoom became a major platform for me. I have also participated in readings on Facebook Live. For example, here is the link to part 1 of the major three-part virtual series, *Afrofuturism and the Black Speculative Arts* in which I participated: [https://www.youtube.com/watch?v=8U41wB4_E5U&feature=youtube]. I highly recommend listening to part 2 and part 3, too. In fact, I think they will play as soon as part 1 finishes playing. There are several well-known poets and writers who participated in the series, including Ishmael Reed, Eugene B. Redmond, Devorah Major, Jerry W. Ward Jr., Ayodele Nzinga, Glenn Parris, C. Liegh McInnis, Tureeda Mikell, Len Lawson, Darrell Stover, Avotcja, Michael Warr, and Staajabu. Dr. Kim McMillon served as the moderator. Additionally, I have participated in a literary conversation with Dr. Glenn Paris and Dr. Lauri Scheyer on a program titled *Writers on Writing* on Facebook Live. A number of these events are on YouTube. After the lockdown in March of 2020, I taught my classes online. I became more involved with teaching in

Moodle. I began to type comments on my students' assignments online. I had long been downloading my students' assignments to grade and entering their grades in Moodle. I had also long been uploading assignments in Moodle. For several years, however, I have entered my students' grades into Moodle and then their semester grades/final grades, too.

DGL: This week I'm preparing for my own classes in literary criticism for the upcoming semester. I plan to ask my students a question about Plato or Aristotle, so I'll ask you the same question. Actually, there are two questions that I like to ask them to help them reflect on what poetry means to them. Here's the first one: Plato in *The Republic* expressed the idea that poetry can change people's lives and that poetry has an ethical function, and this frankly worried Plato. Do you agree with Plato? As a poet do you feel like you can affect the way people live and even change their lives? Or are you more on the side of Aristotle who in *Poetics* argued that poetry is just a way to blow off steam, to elicit an emotional release? Which ancient Greek philosopher do you find yourself closer to you when thinking about your own poetry? Are you changing lives or are you inciting an emotional experience? Or is it a bit of both?

LDM: Yes, I certainly think that poetry can change people's lives, but I do not know why one would worry about it. I feel that poetry changes people's lives for good reasons, such as evoking a greater emotional appeal and enabling people to glean multiple meanings for certain topics and situations. No, I am not certain anyone can affect the way people live, because people must want to change their lives. I do think, however, that poetry can reveal the beauty of the natural world and the richness of people's lives. To that end, perhaps, people would not want to pollute the natural world. No, I do not think poetry is just a way to blow off steam. I believe that poetry has its function in people's lives. I hope my poetry changes people's lives and triggers an emotional appeal in people's lives.

DGL: To what degree do your feelings about poetry align with the Black arts movement of the sixties—Amiri Baraka, Nikki Giovanni, Sonia Sanchez, and others? They seemed to be following Plato's idea that poetry can change the world; that it can bring about social progress and awareness that would help the civil rights struggle. Are you aligned with poets who are using their work to bring justice to the world and especially to the USA?

LDM: Yes, I believe that poetry helps to change the world. I also believe that it is the poet's job to depict truths in his or her poetry. Then, maybe poetry can also help to bring justice to the world. Whenever something happens, people usually turn to poetry. Thus, poetry possibly offers answers to questions that might haunt people. Additionally, poetry can bring healing to people. In short, poetry has its functions in society.

DGL: The second question I like to ask my students regarding Plato and Aristotle concerns where poetry comes from, what poetry is. In another of his dialogues, *The Ion*, Plato describes poetry as a divine madness, an inspiration from the gods above. Aristotle, on the other hand, talks about poetry as a set of techniques and rhetorical structures skillfully applied. Where do you find yourself on that continuum? Do you believe with Plato that poetry is inspired by something beyond your conscious self, or do you find yourself more in agreement with Aristotle—that poetry is about mastering techniques and structures?

LDM: When writing poetry, I definitely think the divine enables me to write poetry. I also think that mastering one's craft enables the poet to write poetry. Additionally, I think reading widely helps the poet to write poetry, too. In short, I think more than one technique enables the poet, particularly me, to write poetry. Furthermore, I think years of working at my craft enable me to write poetry.

DGL: Charles Fort once told me that his poetry comes directly from the spirit world. He definitely seemed to agree with Plato's divine madness theory. Is your poetry spiritual in origin or purpose?

LDM: I like Charles Fort's poetry. I have known him for decades. To that end, I am aware that he writes prose poetry. At times, perhaps, the ancestors speak to the poet. Moreover, I have written poetry which I feel embodies the spiritual in some way. I prefer to let the literary critics analyze my poetry.

DGL: Your first collection in 1982, *Poems of Love and Understanding*, has a very provocative title. Do you feel like your poetry promotes love and understanding among people?

LDM: I hope my poetry promotes love and understanding among people. My job as a poet is to write the best poem as humanly as possible and to write about truths.

DGL: When the great library at Alexandria burned a lot of the wisdom and art of the ancient world was lost. If you were to imagine a future great library were to burn, and you could save only one of your books for future readers, which one would it be? And why?

LDM: In the situation that you have described, I think I would try to save *The Geography of Jazz* because I think it embodies music. I think music has a way of calming people and speaking to people. I hope I was able to get the poems right in *The Geography of Jazz* because I spent twenty or more years working on it. I kept revising the manuscript and taking poems out of it and adding poems to it. If I had the opportunity to save one of the several anthologies which I have edited or coedited I think I would save *All the Songs We Sing* because I strongly believe in the collective voice. The anthology celebrates the twenty-fifth anniversary of the Carolina African American Writers' Collective. Of course, I like all of my books. However, I think I should at least attempt to answer your question.

DGL: Living in New Orleans, I really enjoy *The Geography of Jazz*. Could you tell how this book came about and the role of music in it—and in your poetry in general?

LDM: I have listened to jazz for decades. I really like jazz. I have been performing my poetry with musicians and bands for more than two decades. I especially appreciate rhythm. To that end, I have tried to write poetry with rhythm. Decades ago, some of my jazz poetry appeared in literary journals. Additionally, some of my blues poetry also appeared in blues magazines long ago. Thus, I wanted to work with rhythm and music in my poetry. Yet, I began working on my jazz poetry manuscript that became *The Geography of Jazz*.

DGL: I first came across your poetry in the form of haiku. I remember reading and reviewing your collection *Gathering at the Crossroads: The Million Man March*, in 2003 [*Xavier Review* 23, no. 2 (Fall 2003): 60–63], and recently I taught your earlier haiku book, *Desert Storm: A Brief History* (1993). In these collections of one-breath poetry you seem to be chronicling the African American experience with certain echoes of Richard Wright. Did Richard Wright inspire your haiku? If so, how?

LDM: No, I was unaware of Richard Wright's haiku when I started writing haiku. At that time, I had not heard of Richard Wright. However, I wanted to chronicle the African American experience with my haiku writing. Of course, years later, I read Richard Wright's haiku, though I had already had my idea of haiku through much experimentation and reading Raymond Roseliep.

DGL: How do you keep your haiku deeply reflective of authentic human experience and not overtly political? I'll explain what I'm trying to ask: on the back cover of *Desert Storm*, Sonia Sanchez writes in her blurb that your book is "a searching and sensitive commentary on the desert storm fiasco." I don't find your book to be a "commentary" per se, and I certainly don't feel like you pass judgment on the politics of Desert Storm in it. What was your aim in that book? How did you go about achieving it?

LDM: No, my aim is to always employ the haiku aesthetics when writing haiku, though I try to work my own way. I have long striven toward my own style and voice in my haiku writing. So, I just wanted to write the best haiku humanly possible without commentary. I hope that the reader brings his or her own experience to the reading of my haiku. To that end, you are right; I did not try to pass judgment on politics. I am honored and humbled that Sonia Sanchez wrote a blurb for my *Desert Storm* haiku book.

DGL: Of your many other collections of poetry, *The Open Eye* in 1985, *Forever Home* in 1992, and *A Temple Looming* in 2008, which one of these works reflects you're trying something different, perhaps taking a new approach or taking risks?

LDM: I feel that *A Temple Looming* takes a new approach in the way that I wrote about old black-and-white photographs and the ordering of the poems in the book or the structure of the book. However, I like all of my books for different reasons. A book is like its author's child. For that reason, I do not believe in choosing one of my books over my other books.

DGL: Final question: Who reads your poetry, Lenard? Who would you like to have read your poetry? And, in general, should Americans be reading more poetry?

LDM: I hope everyone reads my poetry, especially because I try to capture the times, the moments, the places, and the experiences that I might encounter. I think Americans should be reading more people to understand the world in which we live and to find meaning. For example, many poets are writing about the ongoing pandemic, including me. Thank you very much for such great questions and such an engaging interview, David!

DGL: Thank *you!*

Lenard D. Moore on the Music of Poetry

Ann Angel / 2021

The interview was conducted in February 2021. Printed by permission.

Lenard D. Moore is known as a haiku master, a poet who captures the aha moment in every piece of work he produces. And he produces a lot. With a pencil and miniature notebook in his pocket, he's as likely to stop in the middle of a walking path and jot down the moment as he is to breathe. His work is bright with images and sensory details. It also provides readers and listeners with the musicality of language, with a moment of inspired blues or jazz within the undeniable beats of syllables and words. Of course, we all know words create beats, but many poets, Lenard included, hear music clearly in the world they illustrate, and they bring that music to their audiences. Through his awareness of music in language, Lenard has purposely set out to bring these sounds to his work. His most recent collection, *The Geography of Jazz*, brings music and musical lives to poetry lovers and those new to poetry. He sat down recently to answer questions about the many ways music influences his work.

Ann Angel: Jim Clark in the *North Carolina Literary Review* said of your most recent collection, *The Geography of Jazz*, that this is a "micro-atlas of the territory of Jazz." He credited your history of writing haiku to explain your ability to hone into specific moments of jazz. Can you talk a bit more about why you chose to highlight moments in place and time?

Lenard D. Moore: I have long focused on a sense of place in my poetry, fiction, nonfiction, and playwriting. I have also long striven to create a setting in my work. Maybe that's one of the reasons why I highlight specific moments in place and time. Perhaps another reason has to do with the influence of music on me. I really believe in rhythm, the rhythm of life, talking, walking, and so forth. I concentrate on music and specificity in my writing, no matter the genre with which I might employ. Additionally, I feel that wherever I travel or visit in some way impacts whatever I write. So, I think it, too, has something to do with why I highlight a place in my writing as well. Yet, timing is a significant concept to me, especially the timing of music and within it.

AA: A 2015 article announcing your North Carolina literature award indicated that in addition to writing poetry you play jazz. Do you play an instrument, and do you play with a group?

LDM: No, I do not play an instrument, but I do consider my vocals as an instrument. I have performed my poetry with several jazz musicians and bands around the country and in Canada. I try to capture the feel of the music. I work with how the music makes me feel, how the music moves me, and how the music seemingly levitates me.

AA: When did you first discover the music in language?

LDM: I think I became aware of the music in the language in childhood because my maternal grandfather used to tell stories to my siblings and me. He was a fascinating storyteller. I also recognized the rhythm of the preacher's sermons at Sunday Services. Additionally, the rhythm of songs and music, which played on record players, eight-track tapes, and cassette tapes captivated me. Moreover, I felt the rhythm of poems which we had to memorize and recite in school. In short, I think all those things were influencers. Then, too, I wonder whether anyone can really pinpoint what triggers such rhythm in someone. I am sure some of it has to do with one's genes. To that end, it is important to consider one's ancestors.

AA: You have said the cadences that poetry sings inspire you. For you, how is that cadence evident in haiku and how does it shift and change with jazz and blues poetry?

LDM: I try to create cadence in my jazz and blues poetry. I think cadence also has to do with one's experience. I write from the Black experience. I incorporate my culture into my haiku and blues poetry. I believe that cadence has to be authentic and lived. Yes, the cadence shifts with my jazz poetry and my blues poetry. With my jazz poetry, I improvise, intonate, modulate, riff, and so forth. With my blues poetry, I employ longer lines, similar line lengths, repetition, rhyme, introduce a problem and later a resolution, and create a particular tone throughout the composition.

AA: Sometimes your tanka and haiku remind me of the opening notes to a musical composition. For instance, you write "first spring rain / the honk of a school bus / before daybreak / all of the silence / in this room." The sounds in this poem are certainly reflective of the musical notes of life. The silence is the silence of a musical rest. Always, these poems contain a scene in the story of a life. How do you believe life reflects or lives music?

LDM: Yes, I believe that life reflects or lives music. Everything in life reflects or lives music, including the way trees sway, the way the sun and moon rise and set, the way tides rise and recede, the way animals rove the earth, the way the wind breathes, the way we breathe, and the way insects crawl and/or fly, and of course, the way the earth rotates, the way the stars produce energy. In short, the whole universe consists of some kind of rhythm, which affects us, revealing how life might reflect and live music, too. Can we really explain how our lives reflect or live music?

AA: Why do you choose to capture the music of a scene, scenes, and in the case of *The Geography of Jazz*, whole lives, in your poetry?

LDM: I wanted to capture the concrete scenes and places rather than abstract ideas in *The Geography of Jazz*. I hope the title itself beckons the reader and reels him or her into the scenes and places of *The Geography of Jazz*. I also wanted to render the illusion of a jazz performance in my poetry. I wanted to place the reader at the jazz performance. I also hope that the reader experiences the jazz performance in my poetry.

AA: A review of *The Geography of Jazz* in *Blair* literary magazine said, "While the poems may not initially signal the rhythms of jazz in their presentation on the page, they convey jazz rhythms through Moore's deft handling of the poetic line and his use of formal techniques including but not limited to assonance, onomatopoeia, and repetition." Can you explain what your goals were with this collection?

LDM: With this collection, I wanted to capture the rhythms of jazz and the miniature details. Maybe the reader can see or envision sweat dripping off the jazz musicians and jazz singers. Or maybe the reader or audience can notice something about the finger popping. Moreover, I wanted to employ as many details as possible. Additionally, I wanted to employ imagery. Most importantly, I wanted to employ music throughout *The Geography of Jazz*.

AA: The same review claimed a newly created poetic form: "This collection also includes a new poetic form, jazzku, an innovation that recalls Japanese haiku and tanka." Is this a form you created? Can you talk a bit about this form and the benefit of using it when writing about a specific musical form?

LDM: Yes, I created what I call jazzku decades ago. I have been experimenting with elements of jazz in my haiku. Then, of course, I have continued to experiment with my haiku writing throughout the years. I prefer for scholars, literary critics, and cultural critics to analyze my haiku rather than talk about it myself. If one knows haiku, then he or she hopefully can examine what I might have incorporated into my haiku. Rhythm or music is one of the most important elements I have incorporated into my jazzku. At times, I have incorporated allusions to jazz artists or jazz musicians and jazz tunes. In addition, I have tried to work with the phrasing in my jazzku. Moreover, I have incorporated the names of instruments in my jazzku. I hope I have included enough details about my jazzku. Maybe others will analyze ethos, tone, diction, meaning, etcetera. In short, I have attempted to merge haiku and jazz into a spiritual dimension that might cull the attentive listener and reader. For more information about my jazzku, please see the interview which Dr. Doris Lucas Laryea conducted twenty-five years ago and published in *Obsidian*.

AA: *All the Songs We Sing* is an anthology of collective voices that speak about a variety of themes including the landscape of the Carolinas, racism, and life's recognizable moments. The title evokes music. As the anthology's editor, how did the music of these poems help you make decisions about the poetry to include within?

LDM: When reading all the poems, I recognized certain elements worked together. To that end, I came up with the title *All the Songs We Sing*, especially because I recognized our collective voices singing in unison as if a choir or chorus. After recognizing the music of the poems, I then focused on their topics. The poems reminded me of blues musicians and singers and jazz musicians and singers. They also reminded me of gospel musicians and singers. In fact, the poems captured the Black experience so well. I am living the Black experience. I am the Black experience. To that end, I tried to create an arc within *All the Songs We Sing*, but I will not elaborate further because I do not want to influence anyone's interpretation of the poems.

AA: You have performed your poetry with the accompaniment of a saxophone, with a guitar and piano, and in front of the Mount Olive community with a symphony. How does weaving your words into music change your poetry and reflect the music of your poetry?

LDM: The music enables me to ensure that I weave it throughout the diction, the language, and the rhythm of my poetry. I want to be in sync with the accompaniment of the instruments. I want to become the instruments.

AA: Many of your poems contain a depth of action and emotion displayed in a few lines. You have a haiku that says,

> after midnight sax
> I contemplate calling her
> in this coolness

You've packed an entire short story into this poem of music, a relationship, and yearning. The reader feels the coolness and the yearning. In your poem "A Black Man Tells His Son the Whole Story," published in *Southern Cultures*, you rely upon history and relationships: "For fifty years I sweat my dues, / wept salt liquor from the blues. / This story I tell wherever I go." The history of a man and a country is also found in your book *Desert Storm: A Brief History*. When you write these poems, how intentional is the depth of the story? How does this depth of story help a poem resonate? And what do you hope readers/listeners come away with from these poems that are life lessons?

LDM: I am delighted to know that you have picked up on my focus on story and history in my poetry. My decades of haiku writing have sharpened my longer forms of writing. I am indebted to haiku, especially because most of my writing consists of haiku. Secondly, I think my writing depicts music: blues, jazz, and gospel. I have also written about other music, but I am referring to my concentration. I think the depth of the story helps to fully develop characters in my poetry, especially blues characters or figures. I hope I am able to fully develop characters in my jazz poetry, too. I think I have been able to fully develop the jazz characters or figures in *The Geography of Jazz*.

AA: In many of the poems in *The Geography of Jazz*, you build the world of a musical moment in longer poems. I'm thinking in particular of "Swinging Cool," which begins:

> The bassist hugs
> the bass, plunks it.
> *Ting, boom, ting boom—*
> the drummer beats
> and booms.

In thinking of the musical metaphor, you're creating music in literary form. Readers end up inside that music. What is it about music that moves you to capture this experience in poetic form?

LDM: I think music helps us to remember. In elementary school, we all read and recited nursery rhymes. I still remember some of them. I want to employ literary elements, musical elements that might make my poems memorable. I think music helps to draw us into the experience. I strive to do the same thing with my poetry, especially my jazz poetry. I hope the reader can experience the poem, the poem's performance, the poem's energy, the poem's tone, the poem's story, and the poem's meaning. I also hope the poem's musical metaphor opens it up more. I also hope my poetry tugs at the reader's ears. When the reader experiences *The Geography of Jazz*, let's see what happens. Maybe it will inspire the readers to see jazz and poetry in new ways and notice how they speak to one another. I believe that is how jazz and poetry infuse experience and transform musicians, singers, and poets.

AA: While many of the poems in *The Geography of Jazz* take readers inside music, others tell the story of musicians and dancers. In "Girl Tap Dancing," you give us that experience through the lines ("She taps, pats, clicks, / Shoes dazzling with checkered floor"). You also tell stories of famous musicians in poems such as "Ray Charles Accepts Honorary Degree":

> With help, he climbs the stage.
> They stand. A community crowd.
> . . .
> King Charles
> rocks back and forth,
> a royal song.

This creates a variety of themes within the jazz theme. What is your purpose to include such a varied experience within the jazz experience?

LDM: I tried to capture the experience of witnessing Ray Charles receive an honorary degree and perform at Shaw University's graduation several years ago. I think *The Geography of Jazz* is about witnessing and experiencing. I worked on the manuscript for more than thirty years. I wanted to get the poems right. Like the renowned blues poet Sterling Plumpp told me over the phone decades ago, he traveled to places to listen to the artists and to write. He was referring to blues musicians, blues singers, and blues artists. So, I wanted to travel to places to listen to jazz musicians, jazz singers, and jazz artists. I have also listened to blues musicians, blues singers, and blues artists, but I put a lot of my blues writing on the back burner decades ago, though several of my blues poems have been published. I have recently returned to my blues poetry project. I have listed Sterling Plumpp here, but I am also aware of the great blues poet Sterling Brown. I am also aware of Langston Hughes's blues poetry and jazz poetry. But, yes, I wanted to incorporate musicians and singers whom I thought would trigger readers' interest. I also wanted to write about the lesser-known musicians and singers in such a way that might trigger readers' interest in them, too.

Most importantly, I wanted to write the book that I wanted to read. I will say that Michael S. Harper's book *Dear John, Dear Coltrane* influenced me.

I go back to his book from time to time. I also like Yusef Komunyakaa's jazz poetry. Of course, I love the way Gwendolyn Brooks developed characters in her poetry. I think a mixture of what I have learned and what I have tried to develop are at work throughout *The Geography of Jazz*. One would have to take a look at Sharon Olds's poetry, A. R. Ammons's poetry, and Rita Dove's poetry for other influences. Then I have tried to create my own style and forms. The jazz experience is so varied that one might not be able to fully examine what is at work in jazz poetry. Maybe the readers will buy the jazz musicians' LPs and the jazz singers' LPs or albums. How do the jazz albums and jazz books speak to one another?

AA: You've served as a poet in the community in many ways. One of the most impressive things I've experienced is that you're truly generous in helping other poets and emerging writers find outlets for their work. This includes serving as president of the Haiku Society of America, creating and serving as director of the North Carolina African American Writers' Collective, cofounder of the Washington Street Writers Group, and serving as the honorary curator of the American Haiku Archives at the California State Library in Sacramento. Why is it important to you to help shepherd new and diverse voices in the world?

LDM: I think mentorship is very important. If we mentor others, then they would not have to struggle as long as we have, regarding writing techniques, the writing business, and teaching writing. Many of us learned as we went along doing those things or occupations. However, I think reading great books of poetry is the best teacher for poets. I also think reading great books of fiction is the best teacher for fiction writers. Likewise, nonfiction writers and playwrights must read great books of nonfiction and plays or drama. It is important to mentor diverse voices so that the whole American experience will be documented. To that end, readers will be able to see themselves reflected in books.

AA: Blues and jazz are music genres that require each musician to weave and juxtapose their own sound into a whole musical experience. Anthologies might reflect this genre in the way many writers come together around a specific theme. This is especially evident in *All the Songs We Sing*. You've served as editor of anthologies in which you've edited a variety of poets. In creating these anthologies, how do you consider the musical metaphor and how these poems will come together to form an entire lengthy composition?

LDM: In our CAAWC workshops/meetings, we lead prompts on specific themes, specific topics, and specific genres. We read our poetry and/or flash fiction and sometimes essays from the prompts. Then we workshop the literary works. Several of the works garner publications, and I read a large selection of each poet's works and pages and pages of fiction and nonfiction. For some of the literary works, I make comments/suggestions for revisions. Then I work on the ordering of the poems, fiction, and nonfiction for the manuscript. Before the process is finalized, I think about arranging the sections of the manuscript. CAAWC members have long published collectively in several special issues of magazines and anthologies. I have edited and/or coedited many projects. So, I think those experiences have helped my editing process. In short, I hope *All the Songs We Sing* works collectively as well as individually.

AA: What do you consider (word choice, beat, etc.) when capturing the language of music?

LDM: I consider word choice the diction in my poetry—the way that words might coalesce to create rhythm. I also consider beating the stressed words as well as the unstressed words that strike a chord somehow to create rhythm. Additionally, I consider the literary elements, such as alliteration, assonance, consonance, internal rhyme, repetition, onomatopoeia, slant rhyme, and at times end rhyme. I have also employed eye rhyme. More importantly, I consider listening to whatever I might want to write. If I want to write jazz poetry, for example, I might listen to jazz. If I want to write blues poetry, I might listen to blues. Furthermore, I consider the feelings I might employ in my poetry. Yet, if I want to depict gospel, then I listen to gospel. Then, too, I pay close attention to the gospel songs that we sing in both choirs with which I participate. I do the same thing whenever I perform my poetry with jazz musicians and jazz bands. I think those are techniques that I employ to capture the language of music in my poetry. However, I pay close attention to rhythm within my prose writing, too.

AA: What excites you about capturing the mood or language of music in your poetry?

LDM: I think what excites me about capturing the mood or language of music in my poetry is that such focus enables me to hopefully create my own distinct voice in my poetry, my own distinct rhythm.

AA: What musical genres speak to you most clearly and readily adapt to poetry?

LDM: My favorite musical genres are gospel and jazz. My poetry, however, reflects jazz in many ways. I think I have been able to capture the feel of jazz in my poetry. Then, too, I have written several blues poems, too, but I think much of my poetry mostly embodies a joyous tone because of my decades of writing haiku.

AA: Did you study a musical instrument as a child? If not, which instruments or forms were you most interested in?

LDM: No, I did not study a musical instrument as a child. I participated in singing in elementary school. I sang in the chorus in high school. For several years, I have thought about taking saxophone classes and piano classes. I have never had the time to do so, mainly because of my teaching and other interests, such as basketball and track and field. I just love the music that flows from the saxophone and the piano. I have also wanted to take photography classes for such a long time, too. I guess I just enjoy taking classes, but I have not taken any classes since graduate school about a quarter of a century ago.

AA: Often poetry is a metaphor for life's aha moments. How is music a metaphor that depicts those aha moments of life in your writing?

LDM: I think music is a metaphor that depicts aha moments because it deals with how we feel and how we will respond to it. Music influences whatever we do, such as breathing, talking, and walking. So, life itself has rhythm. We even have a rhythm to the way we teach, the way we journey, and of course, the way we write.

Lenard Moore: Poet, Editor, Teacher, and Mentor

Dee Clere / 2021

The interview was conducted on March 3, 2021. Printed by permission.

Moore as Author

Dee Clere: I'm dividing the interview into three areas: your work as author, your work as editor, and your work as mentor and teacher. I don't claim to have read all your works, Lenard, but I have read a lot, and, although you write in a variety of forms, the haiku seems to be the dominant one. How did you happen to discover the haiku, and why are you so drawn to this form?

Lenard D. Moore: Wow! Dee, I still think about how I learned about haiku. It was about five months after my term of service in the military ended when I was in my childhood bed with the flu. I guess I had gotten bored, lying in bed. So, I grasped my literature textbook, which we used in my creative-writing class at the University of Maryland Overseas Branch, in Stuttgart, Germany. At the time, it was West Germany long before the wall came down. In fact, this month (January 2021) makes thirty-nine years that I have been writing haiku. I write poetry in more than thirty poetic forms. Haiku is definitely the dominant poetic form with which I write poetry. I am drawn to haiku because I like how it makes one attuned to his or her environment, the natural world. I also like employing specificity, vivid imagery, and concise language in my writing because of the demands of haiku. Moreover, I feel that it is my haiku writing that has hopefully enhanced my longer forms of writing.

DC: At a recent reading, I heard you say that haiku influenced your other works even if they weren't haiku. Could you elaborate on that?

LDM: Yes, haiku has influenced my other works, especially with what I have said to your previous question. I will further say that haiku writing pushes the poet to employ the right words or exact words in his or her haiku. Then, too, concrete details help to enhance one's haiku. Moreover, I have experimented with the haiku form, employing topics such as gospel, blues, and jazz.

DC: Early modern writers, enchanted by the sonnet, but frustrated by its brevity, chose to write sonnet sequences. You have written at least two haiku sequences, *Desert Storm* and *Gathering at the Crossroads*. Why the haiku sequence and not just a long, narrative poem?

LDM: I have written a number of haiku sequences. In fact, the poems in *Gathering at the Crossroads* were taken from my longer book-length haiku sequence. I wanted to try to do something with haiku that I had not seen decades ago. I also wanted to incorporate history, landscape, family, generational, and interracial happenings within *Gathering at the Crossroads*, a collaborative project with the renowned Black arts movement poet Eugene B. Redmond, whose photography is featured in the chapbook. Perhaps I could have written a narrative poem about Desert Storm, but I wanted to employ the lyric. I especially am drawn to poetry with musical elements.

DC: Your comment about being drawn to poetry with musical elements leads to my next question. Your poetry, especially *The Geography of Jazz*, is responsive to and inclusive of other arts. *A Temple Looming* is inspired by photography, and of course, the satire project with Larry Lean and Frank Gross was multimedia. Could you discuss what you see as poetry's relationship to other arts?

LDM: I think poetry's relationship to other arts is essential, especially because songs have words or lyrics; films or movies have words or dialogue; photo essays have words or captions; plays have words or dialogue, monologues, or stage directions. One might think of the 1989 movie *Dead Poets Society*. Another might think of the 1997 movie *Love Jones*. However, poetry oftentimes is incorporated into short stories, novels, plays, and visual art and accompanied by musicians or bands. Poetry is also employed as a memory tool. For example, when we were in elementary school, we learned nursery rhymes and memorized and recited poetry. Twenty-two days ago, Amanda Gorman recited her powerful poem "The Hill We Climb" at President Biden's inauguration. Her delivery was dynamic. So, I consider the voice an art form, too. Four days ago, Amanda Gorman also recited her poem "Chorus of the Captains" with such courage and emotional appeal at the Super Bowl. Again, her delivery was dynamic. I think this poem appealed to the global community because it depicts heroes and sheroes who are healing and protecting others during the pandemic. Maybe my answer is a little long, but I think Amanda Gorman brings even more hope to poetry. We will hear from her for a long time to come. Thus, I think more organizations and companies are focusing on poetry at this time. Maybe poetry will garner other relationships even greater, such as fiber arts, ceramic arts, glass arts, etcetera. I hope so. Wow! That was a great question!

DC: You are, of course, first and foremost, a poet, but you have written some fiction. Do you see a novel, a collection of stories, or creative nonfiction in your future?

LDM: Yes, I am an American poet. I have also had two short stories published. I have written a few other short stories. Some of them are ready to be submitted for publication. I have just been holding onto the short stories. I wrote some of them in the late 1980s. I took a beginning fiction-writing class with Kate Burak at North Carolina State University during the fall 1988 semester. I also took an advanced fiction-writing class with Angela Davis Gardener at North Carolina State University during the spring 1989 semester. I kept trying to register for Lee Smith's graduate fiction workshop at NCSU shortly after that semester. Her classes were always full. Lee Smith still made comments on one or two of my short stories through the mail. Fred Chappell also made comments on one or two of my short stories through the mail. He also critiqued a few of my poems decades ago. In addition, he submitted a batch of my poems to the *Georgia Review*, but the editor did not accept any of them. I did not know he was going to send my poems there. He was just kind and generous. When I taught as a visiting professor at North Carolina State University, I was in a fiction-writing group with two of my colleagues, Nancy Tilly and Sheryl Cornett. Nancy hosted our fiction meetings where we critiqued each other's fiction. A couple of my colleagues, Gloria Bowman and Sylvia Massey, in the late 1980s and early 1990s at the Department of Public Instruction, made comments on my short stories, too. Another one of my colleagues, Kim Horton, told me about the book she was reading. She lent her book, *Homemade Love*, by J. California Cooper, to me. I could not stop reading that book. In my fiction classes at North Carolina State University, I enjoyed reading and studying Bobbie Ann Mason's fiction, Raymond Carver's fiction, and Tilley Olson's fiction. In my graduate classes at North Carolina A&T State University, I enjoyed reading Toni Morrison's fiction, Alice Walker's fiction, Richard Wright's fiction, James Baldwin's fiction, Chinua Achebe's fiction, Margaret Walker's fiction, Zora Neale Hurston's fiction, and others.

In addition, I have enjoyed reading and studying Guy Davenport's essays, James Baldwin's essays, Toni Morrison's essays, Annie Dillard's essays,

Langston Hughes's essays, John Updike's essays, Jerry W. Ward Jr.'s essays, Trudier Harris's essays, Susan Sontag's essays, and Amiri Baraka's essays. In the summers of 2002, 2003, 2004, 2004, and 2005, I worked as a writer-counselor at the National Book Foundation summer writing camps. In my free time, I met with one of the fiction workshop leaders, Norma Fox Mazer, who discussed one of my short stories and critiqued it. I also wrote short stories in the tenth grade. My teacher Mr. Young assigned us to keep a diary and write short stories. During all these decades, I have still been tweaking one of my short stories from high school. Yes, I see a future of my writing more fiction. When I was on sabbatical during the spring 2018 semester, I began a novel. In the 1980s, I also began a novel or novella. Wow, I guess I have given you a long answer. Well, I guess that's my love of storytelling. Thank you very much for such a thought-provoking question.

DC: You write in standard English. Do you see African American poets as abandoning dialect/vernacular poetry completely, or will it remain part of their tradition?

LDM: I think poets employ the language that poems beg to grasp or contain during composition or writing. For example, a blues poem embodies a certain language. I think such language helps to emphasize the message and highlight or develop certain characters within the blues poem. For the twenty-first century, I do not see dialect in much poetry. Of course, language consistently evolves. If we reexamine Paul Laurence Dunbar's poetry from the nineteenth century, we can infer that he probably depicted the way people spoke during that era. A poet must employ the language of his or her era. To that end, yes, you are right that I write in standard English.

DC: Although you write a lot of poetry in traditional, even ancient, forms like tanka and haiku, you are always alive to contemporary poetry. Would you define Afrofuturism and discuss its influence on your poetry?

LDM: Yes, for me, Afrofuturism embodies the past, present, and future. I work more towards the future with my Afrofuturistic poetry. My Afrofuturistic poetry depicts or contains Blackness, which I think is pertinent. In other words, I reimagine certain ideas and concepts in my Afrofuturistic poetry. It is about possibilities. I have also experimented with what I call Afrofuturistic haiku. Before I share an example, I think I would like some of my Afrofuturistic haiku to garner publication.

To finish my answer, Afrofuturistic poetry also incorporates science and technology. At some point, readers will witness my Afrofuturistic haiku. Time is an important element, too. I hope I have said enough about Afrofuturistic poetry. I prefer to leave the analysis of Afrofuturistic poetry to the literary critics and literary scholars, students, and others. I want to write poetry, fiction, and nonfiction. I also want to write plays. I really do not want to spend time analyzing my own poetry. Let me be a poem and hopefully resonate. Thank you very much for your engaging question!

DC: Asking an author to pick a favorite book is like asking a parent to pick a favorite child, but does any book have special meaning or give you special satisfaction to think of? Alternatively, is there any poem or collection of poems that has a back story you would like to talk about?

LDM: I like all my books. Like people, each book has different characteristics. So, all my books are different. Each one has its distinct message, meaning, and music. I cannot pick a favorite book of mine. Let them each tell a unique story. Like children, my books are unique and must be treated that way. I say let them evoke emotions within their readership. Let them contain a multitude of empathy, love, and gratitude. I hope my books will find homes all over the world. Let's see what happens.

Moore as Editor

DC: You have edited about as many books and journals as you have authored. Compare and contrast the two roles. What satisfaction do you find in each?

LDM: When I write a book, I try to create an arc or explore a theme or write extensively on a topic. I write as if there are writerly doors that I must enter and explore and try to discover what cannot be seen. I hope my writing works that way as well as in other ways, such as musically. To that end, I consider the music or rhythm of my writing when I author a book. When I edit anthologies or journals, I examine how each literary work might be in conversation with the other ones. I work toward cohesiveness: theme, subject, etcetera. I hope the anthology or journal, which I might have edited, will resonate. I love editing anthologies and special issues of journals. I have guest edited several journals. The two most recent anthologies I have edited are *All the Songs We Sing: Celebrating the 25th Anniversary of the Carolina African American Writers' Collective* and *One Window's Light: A Collection of Haiku*. My most recent poetry book is *The Geography of Jazz*. I have worked on the manuscript for the latter book for twenty or more years. I keep revising the manuscript. I also kept adding poems and tweaking them again and again. So, I take writing very seriously, too.

DC: What criteria do you use in deciding what works to include in an anthology?

LDM: I select the best literary works, which resonate. I also try to find out whether the literary works fit into a theme. In addition, I try to find out whether the literary works cover the same topic or subject. Moreover, I try to find out whether the literary works work as a complete manuscript. Hopefully, the anthology will shed light on a subject or region or reveal new meanings.

DC: One of your most recently published books is *All the Songs We Sing*, a collection of works by the group you founded in 1995, the Carolina African American Writers' Collective (CAAWC). Why did you find this group and what role has it played in your life and those of other members?

LDM: I founded the Carolina African American Writers' Collective as a safe place to workshop, critique, and fellowship. There is an essay, which I wrote as a tribute to my poetry professor Gerald Barrax, informing about the genesis of the group. However, I think the Carolina African American Writers' Collective plays a significant role in our lives. We also celebrate each other's literary accomplishments. We carpool to funerals. When a member loses a family member, we send flowers. We attend each other's readings, workshops, etcetera. We discuss literary trends and literary markets. We share writing prompts. We inform each other about new books. We assign short stories and poems to read. For several years, we had the CAAWC newsletters. I started typing the newsletter on CAAWC letterhead. Gina Streaty became the CAAWC newsletter editor and redesigned it on the computer. She did an excellent job editing and producing the CAAWC newsletter. I distributed it at our CAAWC workshops/meetings. I also mailed copies all over the country and abroad. In the early days of our CAAWC workshops/meetings, I purchased literary journals or magazines and gave them to the first five people in attendance. We have published as a group on several occasions. We have also read together on many occasions. In other words, we support each other.

Moore as Teacher and Mentor

DC: I've known you in your role as teacher and mentor as much as poet. I know you take teaching very seriously and spend a lot of time working with students and commenting on their papers. Do you ever resent the time this activity takes away from your poetry?

LDM: Yes, I do take teaching very seriously. Yes, I spend a lot of time working with my students. Yes, you have seen the many comments that I write on my students' papers. I like to give my students' papers close readings. I want to help them progress with their writing. To that end, I suggest certain writers and books to read. Of course, it depends upon what areas of their writing I think could be improved. For example, a student might need to focus more on sentence variety or sentence structure in his or her writing. If so, then I could suggest that he or she read Guy Davenport's essays, James Baldwin's essays, Annie Dillard's essays, Toni Morrison's essays, or Gary Soto's essays. When I teach fiction writing, I teach the elements of fiction writing, such as plot, setting, characterization, conflict, dialogue, etcetera. In my fiction classes, however, we work on one element at a time. Of course, we read fiction and discuss it. When I teach poetry, I teach different poetic forms. If one is to become a master poet, I think he or she should at least know the poetic forms and how they work even if he or she chooses to only write free verse. I tell my students that we are building a short story like a carpenter builds a house. After classes ended during the day and into the summers, you and I both worked with our students in the fiction workshop. As department chair of the Language and Literature Department, you also remained on campus to help our students. We both take teaching very seriously. We both also worked on weekends to help our students, too, such as the Sigma Tau Delta ceremonies. I want to be available to assist with the craft of writing.

I remember when I was my students' age, I mostly had to figure things out by putting more time into my work, such as library visits and lab visits. I think it helps if they can discuss their papers with me. All of them cannot always come for help during office hours. During late afternoons, student athletes have practice. The band and chorus students usually have practice during afternoons, too. I always tell my students that I would not assign work that I would not do. In other words, I want to serve as a role model. Thus, they know that I am a reader. Like exercising our bodies, we also need to exercise our writing muscles so that they would become stronger or so that our writing will strengthen. In short, I love teaching. Teaching is what I do. I know I have given you a lengthy answer. I love storytelling, too.

DC: I've known many good creative-writing teachers, but you are the best at getting your students opportunities to publish their own works. Could you talk about why that's important to you?

LDM: I think it should be required for creative-writing teachers to help their students get published. As you know, I include a literary works submission day on my syllabus. I teach my students how to write cover letters and the business side of creative writing. Before the internet was embedded in the classroom, I assigned my students to bring two business-sized envelopes (one for the SASE) and postage stamps. I showed them how to prepare the manuscripts and include the self-addressed, stamped envelope for return postage. Later into the twenty-first century, I taught them how to prepare manuscripts to email. Most literary journals, magazines, and publishers are using Submittable during this time. Before the storyteller in me continues, let me get back to the question at hand. Assisting my students with the publication of their creative writing, I take it very seriously. It is important to me because I know publication helps one to continue the writing journey. I have helped dozens of my students with publications during my decades of teaching. Several years later, some of my former students have invited me to participate in fine arts projects with them. One of my former students has been a department chair in a visual arts department. She sent some of her great photography. I wrote poetry about her photography. She contacted me about collaborating on visual art and poetry project. Other former students of mine invited me to speak or read where they teach. I tell my students that I am always available to help them even after they graduate. I am their mentor. I want them to excel. Once again, I know my answer is lengthy, but I get excited when talking about teaching.

DC: Lenard, thank you so much for sharing your thoughts about writing, editing, and teaching. Even though I have known you for over a decade, I think I learned a lot from your answers. I hope others who read this interview will be aware of the multitalented person you are.

An Interview with Lenard D. Moore

Toru Kiuchi / 2022

From *Black Studies* (*Kokujin Kenkyu*) 91 (March 2022): 110–21. Reprinted by permission.

The interview was conducted through Zoom between Lenard D. Moore in Raleigh, North Carolina, and Toru Kiuchi in Tokyo, Japan, on March 18, 2021.

Toru Kiuchi: First of all, in your first collection of haiku, *The Open Eye*, Lorraine Ellis Harr says in "Foreword," "When a haiku poet has more successes than failures, he can be happy, for each haiku is a new beginning." I agree with Harr. Your haiku "sundown: / a pigeon / still in the street" is a new beginning of something which would happen to a pigeon's world from now. What do you think of my interpretation?

Lenard D. Moore: That'd be nice.

TK: There are nine one-line haiku in the first collection of *The Open Eye*. Japanese are familiar with one-line haiku, which is ordinary in Japan. Thirty-six years ago, when the book was published, is it considered quite experimental?

LDM: Yes, when I began writing haiku, I wrote two-line haiku, too. I don't think I've written any two-line haiku since the eighties. I was writing a number of one-line haiku back then. I was experimenting. They published a number of my one-line haiku. But then I just started to write three-line haiku. I've occasionally written one-line haiku here and there, but I don't think I wrote any one-line haiku this year. I don't do that often anymore. I think there might have been one or two people who write one-line haiku. The second edition of *The Haiku Anthology*, edited by Cor Van Den Heuvel, was published by Simon & Schuster in 1986. The third edition of the same book, edited by the same editor, was published by W. W. Norton in 1999. This second edition, I think, has four of my haiku. The third edition includes only three of them. So, one of them was dropped from the third edition because, I think, my haiku has only three words, too experimental. I have one-line haiku in the third edition, but not three-word haiku. It is "stars / flickering . . . / snow" which came from page sixty in *The Open Eye*.

TK: The thirtieth-anniversary edition of *The Open Eye* has no painting on each chapter of the four seasons. Is there something meaningful with the deletion?

LDM: The artist, Claire Cooperstein, died a long time ago. She might have died over twenty years ago. The artist was older when I was younger. Maybe she was in her sixties or seventies when I was in my twenties. I remember meeting some haiku poets in 1985. Before that time, I only knew the haiku poets in North Carolina. Rebecca Ball Rust is the founder of the North Carolina Haiku Society. She just died three years ago. I think she was about eighty-nine years old. She published my first book, *The Open Eye*. At that time, you know, she was still running the North Carolina Haiku Society, but then they all elected me in 1994. So, I've been a long-term executive chairman for a really long time. At that time, I was the only African American in the organization. We had about eighty-five members back then, and it was open to everybody all over the country, all over the world really. So, Elizabeth Searle Lamb and some others were members.

TK: I would like to know how much influence the haiku by Richard Wright has on you.

LDM: At that time when I started to write haiku, I didn't know about Richard Wright's haiku. I started really early.

TK: Only a small portion of Wright's haiku was introduced in books such as Michel Fabre's biography, *The Unfinished Quest of Richard Wright*.

LDM: But, I think, even before I saw any of Michel Fabre's work, *The Open Eye* was published. I didn't know about his work then. When I found out about Richard Wright's haiku, I really liked his haiku: "In the falling snow / A laughing boy holds out his palms / Until they are white." In fact, I didn't know about any African American haiku when I wrote back then. Because I began so long ago, I was writing haiku in 1982, I didn't know about any African Americans writing haiku. So, you know, I was doing this a long time ago, learning about poetry. How did you first hear about my haiku? You wrote me in 1986.

TK: When I read Jerry W. Ward's review of *The Open Eye*, published in *Black American Literature Forum* [now *African American Review*], I knew you.

LDM: Yes, the journal also published some of my haiku and tanka in 1983. So that was way before I heard of Richard Wright.

TK: I forgot how I got your address when I wrote you. I did not know Jerry back then. No email, no internet in 1986. Maybe through the Haiku Society of America.

LDM: I won the first prize of the Haiku Museum of Tokyo Award in 1983. Then again, I won it in 1994. Then I won it again in 2003. So, three times. And then I won the first prize of another award. I don't know if you know this. I might say it wrong, from *Mainichi Daily News* in Tokyo in 1992; one of my haiku won the first prize for the traditional category for all the haiku published that year. So maybe you can find out my haiku in the issues somewhere.

TK: I have some questions about *Forever Home*.

LDM: Let me show you some. Look at the first edition of *Forever Home* in 1992. Here is the second printing in 1996 with the new cover. So, you didn't know about this, huh? This was published by St. Andrews Press. This was published by St. Andrews College Press. Now it is St. Andrews University. I said "for Bashō" in one of the poems, "Onslow County, North Carolina" on page 47. I knew Bashō's haiku early on. Even though one hundred twenty miles from Raleigh, this Onslow is still my hometown. That's not a city but a county. The university is in Laurinburg, North Carolina.

TK: I am overwhelmed by the fact that Gwendolyn Brooks says in the blurb for the first full-length collection of poems, *Forever Home*: "I feel sure that it's 'just a matter of time' before his validity is recognized as it should be recognized." I have seen Brooks walking in Washington DC in 2000. Her prediction came true as a matter of fact.

LDM: She invited me to a poetry festival in 1983 when I read at the Library of Congress. She was the poetry consultant. That position is now the United States poet laureate. I think Robert Hayden had that position some years before her, too. And Fred Chappell, another blurb writer for *Forever Home*, is well-known, too. He is a southern poet. And then Guy Davenport wrote the introduction. He's well-known, too. He won the MacArthur Award, which is considered a genius grant, and then the *Forever Home* afterword by Fred Chappell. You know the book *Desert Storm: A Brief History*? You see the afterword on page 59? Miller Williams, who wrote the afterword, read his poem "Of History and Hope" at President Bill Clinton's second inauguration.

TK: You said in the speech in 2003 at Xavier University: "It's very important to write in a journal, just jot down those ideas, record or do what Gwendolyn Brooks often talked about was reporting which is what she says she did with her writing and so yes, become a reporter for literature." Could I have some more comments on your literary relationship with Gwendolyn Brooks?

LDM: As I stated earlier, Brooks invited me to read poems at a mini-poetry festival at the Library of Congress. And that was the first time I saw

Michael Harper. He was there. I was one of a number of other poets there at the Library of Congress, Washington, DC. It was 1983. I saw her for the first time and saw her several times after that. She came to our class one year. I took some poetry classes with Professor Gerald Barrax. Gwendolyn Brooks came in to teach a poetry workshop to our class. And it was open for some other people to attend, too. So, I really enjoyed that. And I remember she signed the book that we used for the textbook. She said she really liked that picture of her that was featured in it. And then I saw her for the Furious Flower poetry conference in 1994 at James Madison University. I introduced her to some Shaw University students. She spent some time with them, talking to us.

TK: In the collection *Forever Home*, I am amazed by the impact of one of the poems, "In My Memory of My Grandmother." Does this happen to you in reality or in imagination? If real, how did you make poetry out of the experience?

LDM: It might really probably be about my great-grandmother because she died in 1972. My grandmother didn't die until 2004. And my other grandmother died in 2006. This is probably about my great-grandmother. I just did not say "great" there. You know my brothers and I worked together with our great-grandmother in her fields. Cornfields, peanut fields, and all of that.

TK: What do you mean by "for peace take you like it took me" in "In Memory of My Grandmother"?

LDM: Gosh, this is so long time ago when I wrote it. Maybe she was appearing in the dream. This was so long ago, but I think it was probably a dream because the title is "In Memory of My Grandmother." I wrote this in the very early 1980s, probably around 1983 or something. And then in the next poem "Praisesong: From Son to Mother" I'm talking about when my mother used to do visual art. She used to keep all her artwork under the bed. So that's the praisesong poem. And I was about five, six, or seven years old. I used to pull her artwork out from under the bed and look at it. But I guess when we were born, she had to give up on artwork. And "Pathway: From Son to Father" on the next page, there's a part about my father teaching mechanics. He taught mechanics in the military. So that's what that is. And then, of course, he taught me how to do gardening. I also learned from my great-grandmother and my great-aunt. And one of my uncles, too.

TK: Does your family tradition have something to do with African American aesthetics and the southern culture as I wrote in one of the essays in John Zheng's edition of *African American Haiku: Cultural Visions*, published by the University Press of Mississippi, I showed how your poems are related to your experiences through African American aesthetics and through connections to Black southern culture. Especially, the last line: "Watery eyes stare back, we sit still" in your collection of *Forever Home*, rings true and heavy.

LDM: I guess that says that the kids enjoyed the storytelling so much because when my grandfather would come to the house, we would love to hear him tell stories. I have also talked much in some interviews about how I read books on the school bus in elementary school. We were on the bus, traveling so far away. So, you know those children's books I read, and then my grandfather telling stories, were captivating. To that end, I love words or language. I guess that's how that happened.

TK: I read some similar statements in L. Teresa Church's interview with you, "On Being and Becoming a Writer," published in *Obsidian*. Let me ask you about your *A Temple Looming*. In "Moses," one of the three poems in "An Album of Strong Old Men," you say "Moses, original, black dreamer." This reminds me of Harriet Tubman. Could you have some comments on it if you agree with me?

LDM: I used biblical names for all of them. Three different names, Jeremiah, Moses, and I think it might be one more, Gideon. The reason why I said "Moses, original, black dreamer" may be because he has been an African American in my mind. I'm not sure why I did it. I wrote it a long time ago, in 1995 or so.

TK: The next question is about "but Albert waits branchless" in your poem "A Contrast of Two Lives." I do not understand clearly what you mean by "branchless."

LDM: Oh gosh, I have to look at the photographs to know why I wrote that. The collection is "ekphrastic." Look at the note on the back of the book. Yeah, these ones are based on old black-and-white photographs. Note 1 says, "They were written in response to a 1995 request from the visual artist Sherman Jenkins to work on an interdisciplinary project for two years (1995–1997)."

TK: "Woman" is awestruck to me as you say so toward the end of the poem. You use photographs in many poems such as "Double Exposure" and "Still-Life Woman." The photo is an important factor in your poetry. I believe people such as Sherman Jenkins have something to do with it. Could I have your comments on it?

LDM: But you know I still had to do research, such as finding out what type of clothes they wore in the photograph during that era. I noticed people didn't smile in photographs at that time. There are a lot of things to do when I try to be accurate.

TK: So, you use your photographs in many cases. That's why you said "Black and white photograph" in the first line of your poem "Still-Life Woman" and then "a light-skinned woman wears / a short-sleeved, white blouse." Is this from a photo?

LDM: Have you heard about the word *ekphrastic*? Ekphrastic poetry is based on other arts, photographs, or whatever. So that collection is ekphrastic, but I didn't call it that back then. I didn't know that term. So, I had nothing to do with ekphrastic when I did that project. I didn't know anything about ekphrastic when I wrote *A Temple Looming*. That was just a project we did together. I knew the word years later, maybe only about four or five years ago. Sherman Jenkins is a photographer and a visual artist. We were doing programs for the museum City Gallery of Contemporary Art in Raleigh. There were about four or five poets or writers paired up with a photographer or printmaker or sculptor. All different artists paired up together. We had the art at the museum. We also had the poems. We read. I liked the program so much. Then I asked to see more of Sherman Jenkins's photographs. Then I wrote the book. Yeah, so we presented a program for the museum. That's why we did the project. It was called interdisciplinary. No, we didn't know about ekphrastic. We wanted to do an interdisciplinary project. You should have seen the sculptures. They were really good, too. So, one poet wrote about the sculpture. Another wrote about the printmaker's prints. I wrote about the photographs. We had different poets paired up with different kinds of artists. Yeah, it was a really nice program at the museum. I did say something about the program in the back of the book if you look at the notes. I'm sure I mentioned that, too. Maybe the notes are two pages rather than one. I don't have the book here with me. I thought it was in here. Janice Hodges in the note is the poet who was in the class with me when we took it with Gerald Barrax. And I told her I was going to start the Carolina African American Writers' Collective. She lives in the same county. I think I sent you the essay, the tribute that I wrote for Gerald Barrax. I mentioned Janice Hodges in it. Gerald Barrax was a really famous poet. I studied with him. He was living only about eight minutes from me. He taught at North Carolina State University, where I taught later. I also taught at Shaw University as a part-time or an adjunct from 1998 to 2006.

TK: Overall, do images in the collection have roots in your experiences as a student at Shaw University where the emergence of the Student Nonviolent Coordinating Committee (SNCC) happened among people?

LDM: That was way before I was a student there. SNCC was in the 1960s. SNCC started at Shaw University, in North Carolina in the 1960s. So, I have not seen people such as Diane Nash, Marion Barry, and John Lewis. Only on TV. That was before my time.

TK: I'm interested in your ekphrastic poetry. I understand that ekphrastic poetry is a vivid, often dramatic, verbal description of a visual work of art, either real or imagined. For example, three University of Mount Olive professors worked for the Satire Project, which was done by William F. Gross as a composer, Larry D. Lean as a visual artist, and Lenard D. Moore as a poet and vocalist. You said in an interview, "We just inspired one another and created a wonderful final product." What is the typical difference between haiku or usual poems and ekphrastic poems? Can you explain more about the Satire Project?

LDM: Did you send for a copy of *The Satire Project*? I could have given you Professor Larry Lean's email address where you could have written for a copy. He was the lead person who created the DVDs and the book because he's an art professor, and Dr. Franklin Gross was a music professor, and then, of course, I was the English professor there. We all collaborated. We taught at the same place, the University of Mount Olive. Dr. Gross and I did recordings of my poems during the spring break. And a lot of the poems we recorded on one take. I just went with how the music made me feel. So, I didn't really know I was going to sing some of them. I just went along with the music; however it made me feel. That's how I performed. But Gross is dynamic on that piano. *Satire* means humorous or making fun of something in a humorous way. Like one of the songs, one of the poems I sing, a line or refrain about airplanes always on time, and in reality, they're not. So that's a satire. And then you'll see one of the poems says something about a purple dog. There's no such thing as a purple dog or different things like that. This satire is not a reality, but if you see the project, you will see Professor Lean's artwork. He sent me the artwork, and then I wrote the poems, and then I sent my poems to Professor Gross, who wrote the sheet music. Professor Lean did the artwork first; then I wrote the poems.

TK: Thank you for the link for the exhibit *Haiku in the Gallery* at Nasher Museum of Art.

LDM: Yeah, that's ekphrastic, too. We wrote haiku about some of the paintings in the museum. So that's ekphrastic.

TK: I like your "red dress" haiku ("springtime painting: / a black woman's bare back / in the red dress").

LDM: Thank you. It was crowded. A number of people came to the event. We read from this anthology [*One Window's Light*]. It's the first anthology of

African American haiku, published in 2017. I am the editor, and I also wrote the introduction. L. Teresa Church made this quilt [the cover of the book]. I took the photograph. Teresa wrote an essay in the back about the quilt. I edited this book and created different sections. There are blurbs from Lauri Ramey, Jerry Ward, Ruth Yarrow, and John Zheng. I thought you knew about this. It won the first prize in the Haiku Society of America's Merit Book Award in 2018 for the best anthology published in 2017. Maybe you have a copy at the Haiku Museum in Tokyo. I don't know. But I'll send you the link. I'll send you the link for more information on this. But you know what? I edited a collection of African American haiku way back in 1995 and 1996, but I couldn't get it published. So, it's still just in manuscript form. Many well-known people are in that manuscript like Amiri Baraka, Sam Cornish, Richard Wright, and a number of well-known people. I couldn't get it published back then because they didn't think enough African Americans wrote haiku. So, I compiled that manuscript a long time ago. I wrote about maybe a seven-page introduction to it, but it was never published either. And I also put a collection of tanka poems together in 1994, and that manuscript has never been published. Guy Davenport wrote the introduction for it. It was not a copyright problem. I didn't get a grant. The manuscript was accepted by Jane Reichhold at AHA Books, but I never got a grant at that time. So, it didn't get published. I had that a long time ago in 1994. The next year (2022) will be forty years since I've been writing tanka. When January (2022) comes, it'll be forty years since I've been writing haiku. And I've been writing haibun a long time, too. I don't know whether you have seen some of my haibun in *Frogpond* and *Modern Haiku*. I had a haibun in *Frogpond* way back in the 1990s and then some in *Pembroke Magazine*. That's not a haiku magazine. It's a literary magazine. I'm published in literary journals, too. My haibun might have been in the eighties or the nineties, a long time ago. But if you look at *Journeys 2017: An Anthology of International Haibun*, there are five of my haibun in there.

TK: The Carolina African American Writers' Collective is an important collective. As you said in the acknowledgments of *A Temple Looming*, "This book is for the Carolina African American Writers Collective," the collection has strong ties with many colleagues in the collective such as L. Teresa Church, whom I also know. How is the collection related to the collective?

LDM: *All the Songs We Sing* is the book for the twenty-fifth anniversary of the Carolina African American Writers' Collective. It was published in June 2020. It has some haiku in it. It has poetry, fiction, and essays. The North Carolina poet laureate Jaki Shelton Green wrote the foreword. Lauri

Ramey wrote the afterword. Well, we had a false start back then in 1992. To that end, I had to stop it. The collective didn't really take off the ground until August 12, 1995. However, last year (2020) made twenty-five years. We had the first meeting when we officially started, and the date was August 12, 1995, here at my house. I have details in the introduction here in *All the Songs We Sing*. It will tell you quite a bit, including where we performed and read and taught workshops, and all that stuff. It also includes where we've been published as a group, as a collective. We have a monthly meeting, except during the summer. We take off June, July, and August. We meet in the academic year every year. This anthology here [*One Window's Light*], too, includes five members of the Carolina African American Writers' Collective: L. Teresa Church, Lenard D. Moore, Crystal Simone Smith, Sheila Smith McKoy, and Gideon Young.

TK: I attended the online reading from the anthology *All the Songs We Sing*, hosted by the University of North Carolina at Chapel Hill on February 9, 2021. The collective helps young writers earn grants and fellowships and get published?

LDM: We polish our work at the monthly meetings. We also have writing prompts with which we write new works and read them. We also get critiques. Many of our members have won prizes and garnered publications.

TK: Among several poems in *All the Songs We Sing*, L. Teresa Church's poem "Golden Whistles for Emmett Till" is impressive to me. It starts with "If there was a whistle in Money / worth this boy's life, let's hear it / Break golden streets into pieces, dear God, / shape, shine them to fit Emmett's lips." As Monika Dziamka's review in *Southern Review of Books*, it has not only brought the noise, they've brought the music.

LDM: She and Crystal are good poets. That is probably a minute poem,[1] isn't it? There are all kinds of poetic forms in the anthology. Minute poems, haiku, kwansabas, on and on. All different types of poems in there. You name it. When you get a copy, you'll see all of that in the introduction, and then you'll see the different poetic forms. But there are a whole lot of haiku in there, several haiku. I have a haiku sequence in there, too, dedicated to Sonia Sanchez.

TK: I published an essay on Sanchez in John Zheng's edition of *African American Haiku* and met her in Harlem, New York.

LDM: We brought her to North Carolina in 2007. Dave Russo, Bob Moyer, and I—the three of us organized and hosted the Haiku North America conference. So, we invited Sonia Sanchez. She was a part of the conference. I picked her up at the airport. I took her back to the airport. It was really a great conference. We also invited Kalamu ya Salaam, Tara Betts, and Derek Western Brown because we had an African American panel and an African American haiku panel at that conference, too. So, it was really nice, and it was 2007 in Winston-Salem, North Carolina. You go online and can look at the programs for Haiku North America 2007. I think Teresa and I presented a workshop at that one, too, on quilting and haiku, because Teresa makes quilts. I've written haiku based on her quilts, too. Teresa led a quilt workshop at one of our CAAWC Workshops at our house decades ago. Years later in 2006, DéLana R. A. Dameron and I were at Teresa's house all day. She taught us how to make a quilt. And we made a small quilt, and DéLana got to keep it. That's ekphrastic, too. While we made the quilt, Teresa's husband cooked dinner for us, including baked salmon. However, I've written longer poems, too, from her quilts. I write from all different types of artworks: quilts, photographs, paintings, dance, jazz, blues, and gospel, you name it. I do not do haiga, but I do take photographs, too. Some of my photographs have been published. As a matter of fact, this is my photograph on the cover of this book [*One Window's Light*]. I also write bluesku, jazzku, and gospelku.

TK: Sonia Sanchez writes sonku.

LDM: Yes, that's nice. She is an innovator. I like how she infuses blues into her haiku. I wrote some Afrofuturistic haiku. I have been experimenting much. And then, you see, I showed you haiku in *The Open Eye* which has only three words. So that's experimental. But the editor didn't include it in the next *Haiku Anthology*, though it was in the second edition, but not in the third edition. In the first edition, I didn't publish any haiku. I was still in high school. The first edition came out from Doubleday in 1974, I think. And you know that all three editions came out from the big New York publishing houses. Here's Jim Kacian's edition, *Haiku in English: The First Hundred Years* (W. W. Norton; 2013). I've written poems about jazz in *The Geography of Jazz*. Have you heard of Japanese jazz artist Keiko Matsui and Korean artist Youn Sun Nah? I love to listen to jazz from all over the world.

Note

1. Minute poem is a verse form consisting of twelve lines of sixty syllables written in strict iambic meter. The poem is formatted into three stanzas of eight, four, four, four; eight, four, four, four; eight, four, four, four syllables. The rhyme scheme is aabb, ccdd, eeff.

Interview with Lenard D. Moore

Susan Antolin / 2022

From *Pembroke Magazine* 54 (2022): 192–98. Reprinted by permission.

I first met Lenard D. Moore in 2009 in Ottawa, Canada, at the Haiku North America Conference. An award-winning poet, anthologist, and teacher, Lenard was then serving as the president of the Haiku Society of America. Two years later, when Lenard visited San Francisco to read at the Two Autumns Reading for the Haiku Poets of Northern California in San Francisco, I had the opportunity to attend his haiku reading in the afternoon and the second reading of longer poems later that same day at the landmark Marcus Books on Filmore Street. While I knew Lenard as an acclaimed haiku poet, I did not realize until his performance at Marcus Books just how wide his range was as a poet and how he could turn a poetry reading into a dramatic, riveting performance. Since then, I have read many of his longer poems and have seen him perform his poetry with the accompaniment of jazz musicians. In person, as in much of his work, he exudes warmth and joy. And yet, he is intimately familiar with loss and sadness, has served in the military, and cares deeply about social justice. This is to say Lenard is a poet who brings a wealth of lived experience to his work. The following interview was conducted via email in the spring of 2021.

Susan Antolin: Kevin Young said of the subtitle *Struggle and Song* for his new anthology *African American Poetry: 250 Years of Struggle and Song*: "It wasn't just to mean music in the world. It was to mean music in poetry." Music clearly plays a large role in your poetry, not only as of the frequent subject matter but also in the rhythm and sound of the words in your poems. How did your love of music begin? How would you describe the influence of music on your poetry?

Lenard D. Moore: Like many others, my parents played forty-fives or phonograph records on the record player when I was growing up. One of my great uncles and my great aunt would come over to our house and dance. They would ask me to dance. Of course, I would dance for them. So, I loved music from my very early days. I probably was about six or seven years old. At that time, it was mostly R&B music playing.

In later years, I began to listen to all kinds of music. I have also written two or three poems about p-funk, and two or three poems about rap. I have written numerous jazz poems and several blues poems. In addition, I have written poems about gospel. You are right in that music plays a large role in my poetry. I try to infuse rhythm and music into my poetry. In addition, I work hard on the language that I employ in my poetry. As my poetry teacher Gerald Barrax emphasized in class, I try to incorporate the right words or exact words into my poetry. For that reason, I worked on my jazz poetry manuscript for twenty or more years. I would revise, add poems, and continue tweaking them. I actually started writing the poems for my jazz poetry manuscript thirty-three to thirty-five years ago. Back to the music: another one of my uncles also played LPs or albums all the time when I was in my teenage years. Then when I joined the army, I purchased albums every payday. I listen to those albums all the time. Music is a major influence on my poetry writing. In fact, I try to infuse the sounds of music into my poetry. Kevin Young's anthology, *African American Poetry: 250 Years of Struggle and Song*, is an excellent book. I have recently presented a program with Darrell "Sci-Poet" Stover for the Wake County Public Library, using Kevin Young's anthology. After that program, I presented another program on the art of haiku, using the haiku in Young's anthology. Kevin Young himself is a very powerful poet. I hope that when readers think of my poetry, they think of music or rhythm.

SA: What poets have you admired most?

LDM: I admire so many poets. In my midtwenties and thirties, I often read Langston Hughes, A. R. Ammons, Gwendolyn Brooks, Sharon Olds, Miller Williams, Raymond Roseliep, Rita Dove, and Michael S. Harper.

SA: Are there particular poems that have influenced you?

LDM: There are a number of poems that have influenced me. I really liked Gwendolyn Brooks's poem "We Real Cool," Robert Hayden's poem "Those Winter Sundays," Dudley Randall's poem "Ballad of Birmingham," Michael S. Harper's poem "Dear John, Dear Coltrane," Yusef Komunyakaa's poem "Facing It," Miller Williams's poem "Ruby Tells All," Robert Browning's poem "My Last Duchess," Rita Dove's poem "Canary," Gerald Barrax's poem "Cello Poem," Langston Hughes's poem "The Negro Speaks of Rivers," Paul Laurence Dunbar's poem "Sympathy," Maya Angelou's poem "Still

I Rise," Lucille Clifton's poem "homage to my hips," Nikki Giovanni's poem "Nikki-Rosa," Theodore Roethke's poem "My Papa's Waltz," Elizabeth Bishop's poem "The Fish," Dylan Thomas's poem "Do Not Go Gentle into That Good Night," Wallace Stevens's poem "Thirteen Ways of Looking at a Blackbird," Robert Frost's poem "The Road Not Taken," Marianne Moore's poem "The Fish," A. R. Ammons's poem "Corsons Inlet," Adrienne Rich's poem "Aunt Jennifer's Tigers," Sharon Olds's poem "First Thanksgiving," Anne Sexton's poem "Her Kind," Sonia Sanchez's poem "Blues," and Sterling A. Brown's poem "To a Certain Lady, in Her Garden." There are other poems of Sterling A. Brown that I like, but I have listed this poem of his because I have done gardening for many years. All of the above titles, however, are important to me, because the poems incorporate music.

SA: As the founder and executive director of the Carolina African American Writers' Collective, you have created and nurtured a vital group of writers. In what ways does that community influence your work?

LDM: In the Carolina African American Writers' Collective workshops/meetings, we learn from each other. A different CAAWC member teaches the monthly workshops. We all bring our sensibilities into the workshop settings, which enhance our critique sessions. We all probably approach the writing process differently. To that end, I think the writing prompts, which are assigned at each CAAWC workshop/meeting, are more varied. When we read together, however, it seems like we are a chorus or choir as I wrote in *All the Songs We Sing*.

SA: Writing poetry and making a living are often competing necessities for poets. How have you managed to have a work life that allows enough space for poetry?

LDM: When teaching throughout the year, I write evenings and nights. I have also written in the early mornings. I have written during lunch hours. If no students come to my office during office hours, and I do not have any students' papers and creative writings to grade, I might use the time to write. When I commute long distances, I find that poems come to me. At times, I have pulled off the edge of the exit ramp so that I can write notes or a poem in my journal. When I arrive on campus, I sometimes sit in the car for a few minutes with jazz playing or NPR and write whatever poem emerges. Of course, that means that I must remember the poem.

SA: Some poets can only write in a quiet room while others write in public places with people and music around them. For you, what is the ideal writing environment?

LDM: I do not know whether I have an ideal place to write because I write in all types of environments. I like to go on ginkos (haiku walks). I like to listen to jazz. I love to watch sports. I like to attend readings. I like to visit museums. And I like storytelling. All those events trigger poems for me. In short, I write with jazz playing. I write in quietude. I have also written several poems at the beach. So, I can write in a quiet room as I have many times in the library. I can also write in public places with music and people near me. Anyhow, I used to sit at the mall and people watch. My poem "Greenbriar Mall, East Point" illustrates this point in *The Geography of Jazz*.

SA: Do you write with a particular audience in mind?

LDM: I do not think I particularly have a particular audience in mind when I write poetry. I hope my target audience is everybody. I want to write the best poem I possibly can and hope it is accessible.

SA: You have a way of transforming a poetry reading into a true performance. How have your readings evolved over the years? Are there poets or other types of performers you have drawn inspiration from for the way you perform your poems?

LDM: I am grateful to you for your kind words about my poetry readings and performances. I think I somehow have grown into my own way of performing because I am able to feel the rhythm of the music, including in my poems. I think it is the rhythm which enables me to perform in the way that I do. I am not sure what that might be, because I am not able to watch myself perform. I am able to feed off the energy of my audiences. I think the audience has a way of helping my performances because when they are responding like call and response, I take risks with my performances. I always try new ways of performing. In fact, I perform each poem differently. At times, I sing my poems, too.

SA: You frequently perform your poems accompanied by jazz musicians. How do your poems differ from song lyrics?

LDM: I think the only difference might be that I do not have musical notes or notations on my poems. I perform from the feel of my poems and the feel of jazz when I am accompanied by jazz musicians.

SA: Your book *The Geography of Jazz* includes two poems in the centuries-old tanka form: "Tanka Note" and "American Jazzku." These short poems feel both timeless and innovative. In what ways does tanka lend itself to the subject matter of jazz? Do you envision jazzku becoming a new genre of poetry?

LDM: Decades ago, I experimented with employing elements of jazz in my tanka. I also experimented with the parts of speech in my tanka. For example, in the "Tanka Note" poem, I employed mostly nouns in each line, except for the third one. In the fourth line, I took risks by striving for a duality of effect, such as vivid imagery and contrast at the same time. Hopefully, the fourth line also alludes to race with "the black and white" in it. It is my hope that the line triggers a variety of ways to explicate it.

In addition, I strove for an expansive opening line, which shows our human oneness with music as if it were the natural world. What does the second line "shadows everywhere" conjure with its mystery and eeriness? Like jazz, I tried to establish some kind of atmosphere. Most importantly, I employed improvisation in "Tanka Note." To that end, I did not use any punctuation. Yet, I only use capitalization for Duke Ellington's name. His name is familiar. It also brings history to the poem. In addition, it establishes an era. What does the "Tanka Note" poem reveal about the bookmark? What is the connection between the "piano," the "bookmark," and the "door panel?" In short, I hope the "Tanka Note" poem illustrates freedom in some way. I could say more about the poem, but I hope the reader participates in the poem's unfolding. With the poem "American Jazzku," however, I continued to experiment and strove to create my own poetic form by somehow marrying haiku and tanka, employing music, and trying to create a poem that might blossom like a daffodil.

On the contrary, this poem employs a couple of pronouns rather than nouns like the previous poem. "American Jazzku" also employs anaphora and begins with a long line that grows shorter as the poem progresses. Hopefully, each line flows into the next one as if chords. In addition, "American Jazzku" employs at least three of the sensory perceptions. Moreover, the poem contains sounds and silences. Then, too, it also contains a contrast. The line directly beneath the title establishes the setting. The reader is aware that New York City is known for its jazz as well as other art forms. I hope jazzku will become a new genre of poetry. Maybe others will experiment with jazzku, especially with marrying haiku and tanka. Please consider reading *The Geography of Jazz* in greater depth. Then please consider writing jazzku. I am grateful to you for such a great question. Let's jazzku!

SA: In your poem "Greenbriar Mall, East Point" you reference "my people" in a way that feels warm and celebratory. That sense of lifting up the African American community as a whole permeates much of your work. Is that something you have set out to do intentionally?

LDM: I am delighted that you have stressed what I tried to do with my poem "Greenbriar Mall, East Point." I visited Greenbriar Mall in the East Point community about two decades ago when I was in Atlanta to read at the National Black Arts Festival. I watched the people walk through the mall and observed the rhythm, colors, and tone as if I were a painter. I tried to paint them with words in my poem.

SA: You have also written of struggle and personal loss in your poems. To what extent does the subject matter determine the form the poem will take?

LDM: There are times when a poetic form, which I employ, chooses me. And there are times when I choose the poetic form with which I write. When I lost my daughter, I went to the library daily to write about her. I gave myself a challenge. I wanted to write poetry about her, employing several different poetic forms. I had to teach myself to write in some of those poetic forms. Some of the poetic forms were difficult. I kept working with them. I think I employed more than twenty-five different poetic forms to write poetry about my daughter. She died on my next-to-the-youngest brother's birthday. A year later, I had written enough poems for a book. Some of the poems have been published in magazines, literary journals, and anthologies. I think writing is healing.

SA: In your haiku as well as in your longer work, you include concrete, evocative images, clear language, and a sense of immediacy. In what ways (if any) has your extensive experience in writing haiku influenced your longer poems?

LDM: I think my haiku writing has definitely influenced my poetry writing in longer poetic forms. I also think my haiku writing has enabled me to incorporate vivid imagery, good details, and concise language in my longer forms of poetry writing. More importantly, my haiku writing lends itself to specificity, which hopefully enhances my longer forms of poetry writing.

SA: I know you have made good use of the time at home during the pandemic to write. Do you anticipate any lasting changes to your writing life as we transition out of this long period of isolation? In other words, rather than viewing this stage as a return to the way things were before, are there some aspects of this past year you would like to hold onto going forward?

LDM: Yes, I think the pandemic has enabled me to look more inward. I hope that the pandemic has caused me to write poetry that matters, poetry that will be revisited again and again, and poetry that hopefully will be memorable. I have written tanka sequences, jazz poems, an abundance of haiku, several blues poems, and a number of haibun. In addition, I have written what I call gospelku. Hopefully, I have developed my singing and performing further. I have done several Zoom events, which I learned how to do during the pandemic.

SA: Audre Lorde said, "Poetry is not a luxury. It is a vital necessity of our existence." You have said something similar. At what point in your life did this become true for you?

LDM: I think Audre Lorde was right with that quote. For me, poetry is a way of life. I am poetry. Poetry is me. When I lost my daughter, I turned to poetry. I knew that poetry was a way out of grief. I think poetry should be required reading in all schools. I also think there should be poetry posters in doctors' offices, dentists' offices, real estate offices, hair salons, barbershops, and museums. Maybe it would make a difference in the global community. I am trying to make a difference in the world. Let my poetry sing. Thank you very much for such a probing interview.

Interview with Lenard D. Moore

Sharon Hayes-Brown / 2022

Printed by permission of Sharon Hayes-Brown.

Sharon Hayes-Brown: If you were not a writer, what would you be?
Lenard D. Moore: Well, I have also been an educator for decades. I have been a high school English teacher. I have also taught at the college/university level as an English professor. Additionally, I have spent several years teaching as a writer-in-residence for the United Arts Council of Raleigh and Wake County. I began as a writer-in-residence for the Wake County Arts Council.

SHB: What if it were not teaching or writing in any capacity? What then?
LDM: If I had not been teaching or writing, then maybe I would have stayed in the US Army. Maybe I would have kept participating in track and field. Perhaps I would have continued to do farm work because I really enjoy working the land and being one with the natural world. More than forty years ago, I wrote what I considered to be lyrics. I studied lyrics and liner notes on my own. At one time, I was an administrative specialist. Decades ago, I began doing photography, too. In short, I considered a number of options.

SHB: In your book *The Geography of Jazz*, you so beautifully fuse your passion for language and writing with your passion for jazz in particular. In "Quartet at Smoke" you wrote:

> Congas smack
> in the back corner
> of the velvet-red stage
> B3 Organ pumps
> the bird-quick chords
> in spotlight

I can practically hear the music jumping off the page. You paint such vivid pictures with your prose. I feel that again in pieces like "Intermission, 1956" where you write:

> Lady, you seem starved,
> pastel dress drooped
> from your bony shoulders.
>
> Your face speaks:
> three furrows line your brow,
> your mouth—a parted blossom.

The work here is so reminiscent of your book *A Temple Looming* where portraits are given life by your words. I know that you often listen to jazz as you compose poetry. How does jazz inform and influence your work? How is your writing different with no music in the background?

LDM: When I listen to jazz, it creates a certain mood, enabling the writing to flow too. Jazz conjures various colors, especially blue and maybe green. Most importantly, I try to work with rhythm in my writing. I most often try to also work with vivid imagery. Then, too, I try to work with a sense of place. However, I love to experiment with language and music in my poetry. Hopefully, I am able to employ new techniques in my writing. And yet, I feel that the divine graces my work.

SHB: Please tell us more about your concept of the divine and how that informs your work and your life overall. You have mentioned how faith is something you cannot do without. Were you raised in the church?

LDM: I pray daily. In fact, I pray several times most days. At times, I read scriptures. I have also attended Bible study. I know my blessings come from God. I am just the vessel. Yes, I was raised in the church. In short, I know the divine is at work in my life.

SHB: You are most often referred to as a poet, but you also write essays, stories, and more. Do you think it is important for writers to explore or even master other genres or formats of writing? Is that necessary for a writer to do? Or is it enough to excel at one?

LDM: I think it is important for writers to explore different genres, but maybe one should focus on one genre for mastery. I think it is necessary for a writer to know how to write well—period. At some point, a poet will need to write prose, maybe an essay for a grant applicant or fellowship or maybe a final report for a grant or fellowship. It is also important to know how to write letters well. What about knowing the mechanics of writing an email or memorandum?

SHB: Talk about your connection to and affinity for music. Has it always been jazz for you? What other music inspires you?

LDM: I love music. I especially love rhythm. In childhood, I loved the rhythm of my maternal grandfather's storytelling, the rhythm of the preacher's sermons, the rhythm of the choirs, and the rhythm of playing basketball and running track and field. I began to appreciate jazz more in my late teens and early twenties. I began really loving gospel music. I also enjoyed R&B music and funk music. Additionally, I like reggae music and pop music. I have also listened to country music and bluegrass music. I have also listened to music from other countries and cultures.

SHB: I love the way you link the rhythms of storytelling, sermons, and sports. They are so musical in their own way and remind me of the overall musicality of Black people and how that musicality often works as a unifying force. When you write, do you find the rhythm as the piece evolves, or are you more inspired by an existing rhythm first such as you find in listening to jazz and write around that?

LDM: I think it works both ways. At times, the musicality of our people, our culture, and our histories inspires me to write. Then, too, there are times when a piece I am writing leads me down a musical path or direction. Yes, many times, the literary work that I might write creates a rhythm or opens up in another rhythmic way.

SHB: Writing poetry about jazz seems very meta. So much of jazz is poetic, and so much of poetry is jazz. The connection is very strong. You've fused the ideas of jazz and blues with haiku in particular and refer to this genre as jazzku and bluesku. To what do you attribute the natural fit of music and poetry?

LDM: By incorporating music into my haiku, particularly jazz and blues, I hope to highlight the Black experience and Black culture. I think those elements or musical forms fit my jazzku or bluesku because I am able to experiment, improvise, catch a rhythm, and work with phrasing.

SHB: If you could listen to only one song over and over, what would it be?

LDM: For gospel, I could listen to "Amazing Grace" again and again. For jazz, I could listen to "A Love Supreme" again and again.

SHB: What do those songs do for you or mean to you?

LDM: Those songs are very inspirational to me. They also help to create a calm atmosphere. By listening to those songs, I do not ponder long about the ongoing pandemic or other things.

SHB: Are you a musician? If not, what instrument do you wish you could play, and why did you never learn?

LDM: No, I am not a musician. I have long wanted to learn to play the saxophone and piano. Maybe one day I will get the opportunity to learn how to play both instruments. In the past, I have tried to focus on my teaching and writing.

SHB: Have you written any songs?

LDM: Yes, I wrote a few songs in the late 1970s and early 1980s. I mailed some of my lyrics to a company, which created sheet music and records. Someone else sang on those projects. However, there are some songs, which include my poems or lyrics, on the DVD for the Satire Project. I performed and sang my poems or lyrics on the DVD for the Satire Project. Dr. Franklin Gross recorded me singing for the Satire Project during the 2016 spring break. I have also performed my haiku and longer forms of poetry with jazz musicians and jazz bands.

SHB: Haiku is infantilized to a degree in that it is regulated to children in America. I remember learning about it in elementary school but really only scratching the surface. I think most Americans have a passing knowledge of the art form, but it is only briefly visited in most school systems. Have you observed that? Was that your experience?

LDM: Yes, you are definitely right about haiku being briefly visited in many school systems. Perhaps, it would help to invite haiku poets to teach haiku in the school systems. When I taught poetry in the schools, I always included a lesson on haiku. However, I do not recall being taught haiku when I was in school. We were taught to memorize poetry and then recite it. I feel that more poets could help with the teaching of poetry, though there might need to be workshops on pedagogy.

SHB: In what ways has your haiku writing evolved over the decades?

LDM: You have asked a very thought-provoking question about my haiku writing. I think I should leave it up to the literary critics to examine how my haiku writing has evolved over the many years or decades. I will say that I think the structure of my haiku has evolved through my experimentation with the form, such as my jazz haiku or jazzku, blues haiku or bluesku, and gospel haiku or gospelku. I have also been experimenting with the word *gospelku* itself, such as whether I should use the hyphen between the word *gospel* and *ku* for clarity. Then, too, I have experimented with writing Afrofuturistic haiku. Additionally, for decades, I have experimented with incorporating at least three of the five senses into my haiku for more texture rather than just two of the sensory perceptions. Moreover, for decades, I have also experimented with incorporating more music into my haiku, such as alliteration, consonance, assonance, euphony, onomatopoeia, meter, rhythm, and enjambment. Furthermore, I have experimented with allusion, diction, symbolism, and end rhyme, though rhyme is not usually employed in haiku. So, I have not written a lot of haiku with end rhyme. Yet, I have further experimented with repetition in haiku. More importantly, I try to ensure that I employ imagery. I have employed visual imagery, auditory imagery, tactile imagery, olfactory imagery, and gustatory imagery in my haiku. What can we do with the cacophony in haiku? What can we do with eye rhyme in haiku? What can we do with synesthesia in haiku? What can we do with anaphora in haiku? Those are the kinds of questions that help with my experimentation of haiku. I try to create my own form with haiku. I have long found my own voice with my haiku writing. In short, I hope readers would know my haiku if my byline were not beneath it. In the early to mid-1980s, however, I employed my first name in my haiku. I strive to write my African American culture into my haiku. I have also written a few haiku in Spanish. In 1989, my former Spanish professor at North Carolina State University translated my first book of haiku, *The Open Eye*, into Spanish. I believe it was a Spanish grammar class. After Spanish class, she and I would meet at the library to work on the translations. She primarily did the translations. I would inform her about the feel of my haiku, the aim of my haiku, the subject of my haiku, and maybe cultural references and sense of place in my haiku. I do not know whether she has published her translations as a book. I think she retired and moved away. So, we have lost contact. I think she too is a poet. You have really made me probe deeply into your question. Thank you very much for your question.

SHB: I love how in the collection *One Window's Light* you and the other writers took the Japanese haiku and made it about the African American experience. While some of the themes and subjects are universal, the Black lens is sharp, concise, and purposeful. Talk about the importance to you as the editor to present this work as one that was both universal and particular to African Americans.

LDM: I considered how crucial it was to write haiku about the Black experience and include the poems in the anthology. I thought that I would arrange the haiku in new ways into the collection. I wanted the poems to somehow be in conversation with one another.

SHB: Tell me more about the ekphratic collaboration the Satire Project you did in 2016 with musician Franklin Gross and visual artist Larry Lean. Did the three of you work together on each of the twelve pieces? Or was the art first painted with your words and Mr. Gross's music independently added?

LDM: Professor Larry Lean painted the images or paintings first. He sent his paintings electronically to Dr. Franklin Gross and me. To that end, I wrote poems, which the paintings inspired. I sent my poems electronically to Dr. Franklin Gross and Professor Larry Lean. Dr. Franklin Gross created the sheet music based on my poems. Dr. Franklin Gross recorded me reading, performing, and/or singing my poems. Professor Larry Lean was responsible for creating the chapbook of the paintings, poems, and sheet music. He also created a DVD. We originally met with the leading person at the local arts council who wanted us to create a satire project. Professor Larry Lean, Dr. Franklin Gross, and I created the ekphrastic collaboration the Satire Project. We had an exhibit and performance at the arts council, which gratefully was standing-room only.

SHB: Are collaborations such as the Satire Project the highest elevation of art? Is it the pinnacle of artistry to interpret an artistic idea visually, orally, musically, and wring as much out of it as one can?

LDM: Yes, I think collaborations are great because of the sense of discovery. I also think collective voices work best in the arts. Of course, I love working on my own projects, too, but there is something fascinating about collaborations.

SHB: Have you worked on ventures similar to the Satire Project? Would you like to do more collaborations like this?

LDM: Yes, I have done several other collaborations, but they were slightly different. I have also taught interdisciplinary courses. I certainly would like to do more collaborations.

SHB: You were the first African American elected to lead the Haiku Society of America. What did that mean to you? What do you think it meant to the other members of the organization?

LDM: Yes, I was (the first) African American elected president of the Haiku Society of America. It meant that I really wanted to represent the organization well. I wanted to listen well to the membership and advocate well. I also wanted to inform others about the Haiku Society of America and American haiku. For example, I participated on a panel at the Haiku International Association's twentieth anniversary conference, in Tokyo, Japan, in November of 2009. I also participated at the Haiku North America Conference in Ottawa, Canada, in 2009. I served two terms as president of the Haiku Society of America (2008 and 2009). To that end, I traveled all over this country, presiding over the Haiku Society of America quarterly meetings. The regional coordinators organized programs for the quarterly meetings. There were presentations, readings, workshops, etcetera.

SHB: Did you feel any resistance to your election because you were African American? Or was that a nonissue?

LDM: I do not think there was resistance, but you never know what could happen. Many people, especially the Executive Committee, helped along the way.

SHB: Tell me about the Carolina African American Writers Collective (CAAWC), also known as the Collective. You've been together for twenty-five years now, and it is a place for writers to gather, workshop, publish, and perform readings. Was this always the plan?

LDM: When I started the Collective or CAAWC, I did not know where it would lead. We have a great group of poets and writers who all wanted a safe place for our work. In the beginning, I purchased literary journals for each CAAWC workshop or meeting and gave them to the first five people who arrived at my house for the workshops or meetings. There also was an assortment of food available for the workshop participants. Additionally, I typed newsletters for each meeting and distributed them. I also mailed copies of the newsletters throughout this country and abroad. Years later, Gina Streaty took over as the CAAWC newsletter editor and created them on the computer. She designed, typed, and printed them. Then she ensured that I received a stack of the newsletters for each CAAWC workshop or meeting. I also mailed copies of the CAAWC newsletter to as many people and places as possible. We no longer produce a newsletter, but we distribute literary news electronically via our listserv.

SHB: To what do you attribute CAAWC's longevity? Have the dynamics of the group changed significantly over the years?

LDM: I think (there are) certain changes in the way we hold CAAWC workshops or meetings. For several years, we have incorporated writing prompts into our workshops. We have also had critique sessions as part of our workshops. We also distribute literary news, literary markets, and celebrate each other's literary accomplishments. During the fall 2020 season, we shifted our CAAWC workshops or meetings to the zoom platform.

SHB: How does one gain membership into the Collective?

LDM: At first, we accepted whoever had an interest in writing poetry, fiction, nonfiction, and plays. Our membership keeps growing. So now there is an application process, but we are not seeking new members currently. We are trying to help our current memberships with workshopping, teaching, writing, publishing, and reading.

SHB: What is next for the Collective? Are there any new directions you would like to take with the group?

LDM: I hope for the Collective to do more collaborations. As far as new directions, we might do more collaborations with museums, community centers, or cultural centers. And yet, we must see where technology might lead us as well as new developments in the arts.

SHB: Why is it important for writers to join writing groups? Can one achieve great heights and continued growth as a writer without one?

LDM: I think it is important for writers to join writers' groups for workshopping and critiquing literary works. I also think the collective voice can resonate much stronger.

SHB: Workshopping is so important when a writer is developing new work. I think it helps a writer get out of their own head to receive valuable feedback, but what, if any, do you think are some of the challenges of working with a group when creating?

LDM: If you create a family atmosphere, then I do not think there are many challenges, especially if we all leave our egos behind for the workshopping.

SHB: You've spoken about the importance of reading historical as well as contemporary works to inform one's own work as a writer. I recently heard Brit Bennett, author of *The Mothers* and *The Vanishing Half*, say something similar about having her work be in conversation with previous iconic writers whose work she admires. Can you speak about the fine line of honoring, drawing a connection with, or sampling even without being imitative of another's work?

LDM: Well, I don't know about the sampling because I believe in creating one's own work. However, I do believe in being inspired by other writers. I also believe in honoring ancestors. Moreover, I think reading other writers can be the best way to learn the craft of writing.

SHB: As a writer, are you always reading for inspiration or looking for ways to elevate your craft? Are you a multireader? What are you reading now?

LDM: No, I do not think I usually have to look for inspiration. Somehow inspiration finds me. Of course, I am always reading. Yes, I am a multireader. For example, I have been reading *The Poetry of the Blues*, by Samuel Charters; *On the Road Again: Photo Essays on Famous Literary Sites in Japan*, by John J. Han; *Bad Men: Creative Touchstones of Black Writers*, by Howard Rambsy II; and *Cruising Weather Wind Blue*, by Earl S. Braggs. I have also read some of the poems in *African American Poetry: 250 Years of Struggle & Song*, edited by Kevin Young.

On November 5, 2020, I purchased a copy of *Kindred*, by Octavia E. Butler. I look forward to reading her work more closely.

SHB: What one book would you say that anyone who wants to strengthen their writing should read?

LDM: I have enjoyed reading *Patterns of Poetry: An Encyclopedia of Forms*, by Miller Williams.

SHB: What does *Patterns* offer that other books do not in terms of honing one's writing craft?

LDM: I really like all the different poetic forms explained in *Patterns of Poetry*. I also appreciate the poems, which are included as examples in *Patterns of Poetry*. For me, it is the book that I always reread. In fact, I have been reading and reading *Patterns of Poetry* since the late 1980s.

SHB: What are some misconceptions about haiku?

LDM: I think one of the main misconceptions is the five-seven-five structure for English-language haiku.

SHB: You have discussed how you no longer focus on counting syllables when creating haiku. Some would say that the structure of five, seven, five is a necessary component of the art form, but you push against that quite successfully. If it is not that structure that makes a haiku what it is, what would you say are the defining or essential qualities? How far can the boundaries or rules be bent before it is something else entirely?

LDM: Contemporary haiku poets do not adhere to the five-seven-five structure. I remember once seeing a five-seven-five structure book left on the book table or auction table at a haiku conference. In other words, no one was interested in purchasing that kind of book. I encourage you to read the haiku poets who comprise the American haiku movement. I think it depends upon the poets who might bend the rules in such a way that their haiku are still successful. One must first study haiku for years to know haiku well. Then one can experiment with bending the haiku rules. By the way, the word *haiku* can be both singular and plural.

SHB: What then are the defining qualities of haiku? How does one know one is reading haiku as opposed to other poetry forms? Would you say that the five-seven-five structure no longer even has a place in haiku?

LDM: When one has studied and written haiku for several years, then I think he or she would understand the defining qualities of haiku. For one to know that he or she is reading haiku as opposed to other poetry forms, I suggest reading *The Haiku Anthology*, third edition, edited by Cor van den Heuvel, and *Haiku in English: The First Hundred Years*, edited by Jim Kacian, Philip Rowland, and Allan Burns. Both books are published by Norton. No, contemporary haiku poets do not adhere to the strict five-seven-five structure.

SHB: The pandemic has made people connect with nature in a different way. Outside is supposedly the safer space to convene, so people are meeting with others in those outdoor spaces. Many have more time to be outdoors, whether it be through walks, gardening, or just finding safer spaces to meet with others. Have you found this to be true for yourself? If so, how has it affected the way you write?

LDM: Of course, it is recommended for us to be outdoors more, due to the pandemic. Haiku poets, however, have long been including a ginko (haiku walk) to write haiku. When participating in a ginko at the North Carolina Haiku Society Annual Haiku Holiday Conferences, I have sometimes returned to the meeting place with twenty-five newly written haiku. In short, I have always been able to write haiku on a ginko.

SHB: Haiku is typically closely connected with nature. I know that gardening has been one way you've made a connection with nature. Do you still garden or make a concerted effort to engage with nature today?

LDM: I have stopped gardening about four years ago but will probably garden again. I have gardened for decades. Yes, I have always listened to birdsong, crickets, bullfrogs, breezes, ocean waves, and so forth. I have long viewed the moon, gazed at the celestial stars, and watched sunrises and sunsets. I go on walks from time to time, viewing wildflowers and trees. I watch squirrels, rabbits, and deer.

SHB: That sounds like a poem itself! Why did you stop gardening? Has the pandemic affected the way you commune with nature?

LDM: During the past decade, I planted and tended a garden for my parents. During the spring and summer months, I traveled home about weekly for a number of years so that I could take care of the garden. My father also loved gardening. He was older. Therefore, I decided to plant a garden for them. My father would sit on the back porch and watch the garden. He would also look at the plants and I think water them from time to time. I think I stopped planting the garden about five years ago because I am now older. My mother did not like for me to be out in the sun for too long. I listened to that advice because I am now in my sixth decade. I have not really thought about that question, but I guess the pandemic has affected the way that I commune with nature in a small way. I have not been able to go on my usual ginko. However, I still observe birds, squirrels, rabbits, trees, wildflowers, etcetera.

SHB: You've spoken on how a Black writer is Black first and a writer second. What then is the responsibility of the Black creative in terms of creating content? How is it different from the responsibility of non-Black creatives?

LDM: I think it is important for the Black writers to write about the Black experience and culture because we are the Black experience and culture. We live it. We know it. It also is important to write about truths.

SHB: Please explain what you mean about truths. Are you speaking of personal truths or general truths as the writer sees them?

LDM: I am speaking of my truths as well as to the truths of what I might write. If I am writing about a political issue or social issue, I hope I am still able to write about truths.

SHB: Which contemporary writers do you think are the best at carrying forward the African American literary torch?

LDM: I think writers like Natasha Trethewey, Honoree Fannone Jeffers, Raina J. Leon, Chantal James, Evie Shockley, A. Van Jordan, John Holman, Tony Grooms, and Kevin Young would be great at carrying forward the African American literary torch.

SHB: What is your favorite book and why? When did you first read it?

LDM: My favorite book is probably the dictionary because I love learning new words. Forty years ago, when I was stationed in Stugartt, Germany, I constantly read the dictionary. I also enjoy reading scriptures.

SHB: Do you have a favorite scripture? If so, why is it meaningful to you?

LDM: Yes, my favorite scripture is the following one from Philippians 4:13: "I can do all things through Christ which strengtheneth me." It is meaningful to me because it gives hope and encouragement to me. To that end, I know that I can do whatever I put my mind to doing.

SHB: What books in African American literature can we not do without?

LDM: There are too many great African American books to name here. Perhaps if I list the *Norton Anthology of African American Literature*, I think it will cover a lot of ground. And yet we cannot do without *The Weary Blues*, by Langston Hughes; *Native Son*, by Richard Wright; *For My People*, by Margaret Walker; *The Bluest Eye*, by Toni Morrison; *The Color Purple*, by Alice Walker; *Their Eyes Were Watching God*, by Zora Neale Hurston; *Annie Allen*, by Gwendolyn Brooks; *Thomas and Beulah*, by Rita Dove; *The Fire Next Time*, by James Baldwin; and *Dear John, Dear Coltrane*, by Michael S. Harper.

SHB: You have mentioned that you write in longhand either in journals or on loose pieces of paper. Does the connection of an actual pen or pencil to paper make a difference in how you process words as you write? Do you ever write on the computer? If so, how is that different for you?

LDM: Yes, I feel that my writing flows best from brain to hand whenever I use longhand to write my literary works. I do not usually write on the computer. I might have written that way once or twice but not for very long. Longhand writing feels more natural for me. In short, I longhand my writing and then type it. I really enjoy the revision process.

SHB: What other nonliterary, nonacademic pursuits do you enjoy?

LDM: I enjoy photography. I take a lot of photos of people, the natural world, and cultural events. Some of my photography has been published in magazines and printed on posters. I also enjoy singing. I am a member of two choirs. I have also performed with jazz musicians and jazz bands. Additionally, I love sports, especially basketball and track and field. Of course, I love watching all kinds of sports, especially during the Olympics. Moreover, I love visiting botanical gardens, art museums, and history museums. Furthermore, I love storytelling.

SHB: You have said that you hope that African American haiku will become a part of the American literary canon. How far is that from being a reality? How will we know when that has been achieved? What will that mean?

LDM: I am not certain how far it is from becoming reality. I think when we begin seeing more African American haiku featured in textbooks, taught in the classrooms, and sold in bookstores, then maybe it will be achieved. What about African American haiku contests? What about African American haiku conferences? What about African American haiku readings? What about collaborations with African American haiku?

SHB: How has the Black Lives Matter movement affected your writing? Are you working on any projects that particularly speak to the movement?

LDM: I have written haiku and tanka, depicting the Black Lives Matter movement. I am always working on various projects.

SHB: You have won so many awards. Which has been the most meaningful to you? Is being awarded for your work important to you?

LDM: I have been blessed to win a number of awards. Wow! That is a very tough question. I think the North Carolina Award for Literature marks a turning point for me. The Haiku Museum of Tokyo Award (1983, 1994, and 2003) is very important to me. I have been blessed to thrice receive the award. Then, too, the Margaret Walker Creative Writing Award is important to me. The Shaw University Alumni Achievement Award is important to me. Yet, I feel that my other awards are important, too, such as the Indies Arts Award, the Tarheel of the Week Award, the Furious Flower Laureate

Ring, and the Honorary Curator of the American Haiku Archives at California State Library in Sacramento.

SHB: Do you consider yourself a writer who teaches or a teacher who writes?

LDM: Wow! That is a very interesting question. Although I was a writer many years before teaching, perhaps I am still a teacher who writes. I love the teaching profession. When I teach, I also learn. I learn from my students, too. To that end, teaching is a give-and-take profession for me.

SHB: Say more about teaching being a mutual experience.

LDM: I think one way of learning happens during class discussions, especially when my students begin to ask questions. Some of their points of view help me to see certain topics in a new light. My students trigger me to want to enhance my lesson plans further. I like to engage my students with various assignments. I also like to provide opportunities for cooperative learning and experiential learning. When I hear from my students years later, and they inform me what they are doing and what they remember from my class, I am honored and humbled. I hope I have in some way made a difference in the world.

SHB: Do you feel connected with hip-hop and the inherent poeticism of rap music? Could you see yourself doing a collaboration with any rappers? If so, with whom and in what ways?

LDM: I feel somewhat connected because hip-hop was part of my late daughter's generation. I listened to some of the music that she played. In fact, I purchased the CD player and radio all-in-one system for her. I also purchased music CDs for her almost every payday. I like what the rapper Common is doing with rap. Because of my students, I think I know a little bit of what might be happening with rap music but not too much. In my youth, my friends and I mostly listened to gospel music, R&B music, and funk music.

SHB: You have mentioned the impact your grandfather Luther T. Pearson had on you with his storytelling as you were growing up. Were these stories fiction, family folklore, or something else?

LDM: Perhaps it was a combination of those categories, or maybe they were something else. I am not sure, but my grandfather told captivating stories. His storytelling was great!

SHB: Did your grandfather live to see your success as a writer?

LDM: I told him about some of my writing. I also told my grandfather that I wrote poetry about him as well as my grandmother. In fact, my grandmother wrote traditional or formal poetry.

SHB: Do you think you would not have been a writer without the rich oral landscape that surrounded you in your youth?

LDM: It is possible, though I read books on the school bus when I was in elementary school.

SHB: You have said that the attention to language in haiku has strengthened your writing in longer forms of poetry. Can you speak more on how the focus on an economy of words such as what haiku demands, inspires, and improves your longer work?

LDM: I think the conciseness of language from writing haiku has enhanced my longer forms of writing. I also think the precision of imagery through writing haiku has enhanced my longer forms of writing. Additionally, I think the focus on specificity in my haiku writing has further enhanced my longer forms of writing. When I write in longer forms, I think I am still engaging my haiku mind.

SHB: You are so masterful in several Japanese poetic forms. Are there any other aspects of Japanese culture that intrigue you?

LDM: Yes, I love Japanese fashion, cuisine, tea ceremonies, and architecture. I also appreciate ikebana (Japanese flower arranging).

SHB: Did writing haiku draw you to the culture, or was that affinity already there? Have you been to Japan?

LDM: Yes, I think haiku helped to draw me closer to the Japanese culture. Yes, I have been to Japan. In late November of 2009, I participated on a panel at the international symposium on haiku for the Haiku International Association's twentieth anniversary in Tokyo, Japan. I also participated in a renku session. Moreover, I visited historical sites, such as Big Buddha, etcetera.

SHB: Writers know that rewriting is real writing. You have spoken about your penchant for rewriting. How do you know when a piece you've written is done? Do you still rewrite pieces after they are published?

LDM: I do not think a writer really knows when a literary work is finished. When I feel a literary work resonates, then I let it go out to find a home or publication, and a readership and/or an audience. It could be an audience of listeners because I sometimes perform my work. I also listen to the rhythm of my writing and how it might create meaning. Additionally, I try to create a sense of place in my work.

SHB: Talk more about creating a sense of place when you write. I feel that you do such a great job of crafting that space. Is the space there when you begin to write, or do you have the concept of the piece first and fit it into a specific place?

LDM: I try to employ lots of details, vivid imagery, and establish a setting in my writing. In fact, I strive for texture in my writing by employing the five senses. Additionally, I strive to name things in my writing, such as wheelbarrow, swing blade, outhouse, packhouse, barn, etcetera. I think such naming of things in my writing will enable the reader to hopefully picture or envision the setting, the place, and the era. Those are just some of the techniques or elements that I might employ in my writing. What about developing characters? There are times when I develop characters in my writing.

SHB: What is your writing process? Do you write daily?

LDM: Whenever I decide to write or am inspired to write, I simply write. I write longhand first. Then I type whatever I write. After typing my work, I revise it again and again. I usually only write to prompts in our CAAWC workshops or meetings. I write as often as possible. I have written daily for long stretches of time: months and years.

SHB: What books of poetry would you recommend to the reluctant poetry reader? What should one start?

LDM: Several of the books I have already listed are poetry books. Kevin Young has edited a new book titled *African American Poetry: 250 Years of Struggle & Song*. There also is the book *Angles of Ascent: A Norton Anthology of Contemporary African American Poetry*. For African American haiku, I hope poetry readers will consult *One Window's Light*.

SHB: I am very sorry for the loss of your daughter Maiisha in 2004. One of your most poignant pieces was the haiku you wrote after her passing:

> hot afternoon
> the squeak of my hands
> on my daughter's coffin

I can imagine how that squeak probably sounds as clear and resonates as strongly today as it did all those years ago. In "The Way It Happened" you so eloquently wrote, "That awful squeak pierced a door into the house of memory." How did Maiisha's passing impact your work? How long after her death were you able to write anything, particularly about the event itself?

LDM: I started writing immediately about Maiisha after her funeral because that squeak from my hands haunted me. So, I had to write that haiku. I am blessed that I wrote the haiku. I wrote many haiku about her. I would visit her grave and write haiku in my journal. To that end, several of my haiku about those gravesite visitations were placed in a number of haiku magazines. Additionally, I wrote many longer poems about Maiisha because I went to the library daily or almost daily to write. I challenged myself to write poems in more than twenty-five different poetic forms. I have also had several of those poems published in magazines and anthologies. I think my writing shifted during that time. Maybe that time enabled me to somehow incorporate much emotional energy into my poetry. I know I wrote myself through the healing process.

SHB: If your tombstone only gets one word, what would it be?

LDM: Maybe the one word could be Father or Author or Veteran.

SHB: What is next for you? What else would you like to do creatively? What else would you like to do that may not be so creative?

LDM: I do not know what is next for me. I have told others that I have turned the pandemic into a home writing retreat for myself. I also said that in a radio interview several months ago. I have written several poems about the pandemic. I know that the pandemic will end one day. Meanwhile, I am writing and writing. I know I would like to take photography classes, piano classes, and saxophone classes. I hope to do more collaborations. I enjoyed collaborating with other artists.

SHB: Why do we need poetry?

LDM: I need poetry because it helps me to learn more about myself. It also helps me to find meaning in the world. More importantly, poetry enables me to document our history, our culture, and the natural world. Additionally, I think poetry can help to bring about change. If we document the beauty of the natural world, then maybe we can help to preserve oceans, rivers, lakes, creeks, streams, animals, plants, trees, and the earth. Moreover, maybe poetry can help us to treat one another respectfully. We also need poetry for collaborations, especially with music, visual art, storytelling, plays, novels, theater, and films. The recitation of poetry can help with memorization. Furthermore, poetry reports the news, such as the COVID-19 pandemic. Thank you very much for such an engaging interview!

Building Poems Like a Carpenter: Interview with Lenard D. Moore

Lauri Scheyer / 2022

From *Valley Voices: A Literary Review* 21, no. 2 (2021): 35–48. Reprinted by permission of *Valley Voices: A Literary Review*.

Lauri Scheyer: Thank you for agreeing to participate in this interview, Lenard. I'd like to begin by framing my opening thoughts and then pose a sequence of related questions. My focus will be on the areas of your creative practice that I think may have been somewhat overlooked and would benefit from more critical inquiry: your use of diverse forms that are associated with Anglo-American or Eurocentric conventions. As a poet, you are strongly associated with Eastern traditions, and especially forms and themes connected to Japan, though surely you—as well as other renowned African American poets, such as Richard Wright, Etheridge Knight, and Sonia Sanchez, among others—have made forms such as haiku and tanka your own. But in fact, throughout your career, you also have written powerfully in numerous forms more closely associated with the past and present of the Western tradition. For example, you have used many conventional forms from the Anglo-American canon. You have written extensively in free verse. You also have radically redesigned and repurposed forms such as haiku by extending or combining them and using unconventional themes. I am thinking, for example, of the opening series in *A Temple Looming*, where you use a series of extended haiku to create a type of persona poem in your three-part "An Album of Strong Old Men," which includes portraits of Jeremiah, Gideon, and Moses. You have written in what I see as an imagist-objectivist tradition, where you combine haiku's close attention to detail with a modern and postmodern image-oriented impulse to create action by stripping down poetic trappings, where I also see the influence of Pound and Williams. You often write in couplets. That's the background of my thinking for the interview I'm honored to conduct with you. Here are my questions, but please feel welcome to take them in other directions or provide answers to important relevant questions that I've failed to ask.

While you have clearly worked to ingeniously adapt Asian forms and have written extensively in many Western forms, including free verse as well as conventional structures, why do you think the great majority of critical attention has focused on your haiku?

Lenard D. Moore: I am grateful to you for this interview. I think much of the critical attention has focused on my haiku rather than my free verse and other poems in the various Western forms because about forty years ago (or forty years in four more months) there were not many African American poets writing and publishing haiku. When I started writing haiku, I wrote haiku about my hometown, farm work, gardening, and the natural world. Early on, I also infused jazz and blues into my haiku writing. In addition, I wrote haiku about gospel or gospel haiku. Moreover, I wrote travel haiku. Then, too, I experimented with the haiku form. At the time, I was unaware of Sonia Sanchez, Richard Wright, Etheridge Knight, and James Emanuel. I submitted my haiku to many foreign magazines and literary journals as well as many magazines and literary journals throughout this country. I was especially thrilled that my haiku received acceptance in Japan. To that end, my haiku appeared in *Mainichi Daily News* (Japan), *Outch* (Japan), *New Cicada* (Japan), *Soun* (Japan), *Ko* (Japan), *HI* (Japan), and more. You are already aware of my ghazals, blues poems, and jazz poems. I have also written a few Afrofuturistic poems, including Afrofuturistic haiku. I am consistently experimenting with my poetry. Decades ago, I wrote a couple of shaped poems or concrete poems. Of course, I have numerous poems that are unpublished.

LS: Could you please comment on your poetic practice, especially in relation to Western traditions and influences? I realize that these practices are not separate from your writing of haiku, and yet I imagine there are divergences in your techniques, goals, and motivations.

LDM: I write as often as possible, sometimes several poems in a single day. I must tell you that I especially like the revision process, though many of my final drafts are not similar to the first drafts. I write until the poem emerges in a rhythmic way because I want my poems to sing. I love music, striving to incorporate it into my poetry. Then, too, I love the concept of imagery. I also strive to incorporate vivid imagery, auditory imagery, tactile imagery, and olfactory imagery. I believe that figurative language is the key to writing effective poetry. And yet, I must experiment with my poetry to somehow write a poetry that is distinct and textured.

LS: Music is such a prominent presence in your poetry, and that includes references to many different musical styles. As just one of many examples, I'm thinking of your poem "The Poet Man/Spirit Woman." Could you please discuss in detail the role of music in your life and how music and musicality are manifested in your poetry?

LDM: Yes, music is certainly prominent in many of my poems. I started listening to music very early in my life. In fact, I listened to the choirs at my hometown church. When I was a teenager, I visited other churches and enjoyed listening to gospel songs. I also listened to R&B music early in life, such as the Supremes, Aretha Franklin, Marvin Gaye, Gladys Knight and the Pips, Smokey Robinson and the Miracles, the Jackson Five, and several others. In my teen years, I also listened to funk music and disco. I enjoyed all kinds of music. For example, I listened to the Eagles, ABBA, the Beatles, the Osmonds, the Steve Miller Band, Carly Simon, Rufus and Chaka Khan, Denise Williams, Stephanie Mills, the Jones Girls, A Taste of Honey, Rose Royce, Isley Brothers, George Clinton, Parliament-Funkadelic, Bootsy Collins, Ohio Players, Dramatics, Earth, Wind & Fire, and so forth. I have also listened to blues musicians and blues singers, such as Koko Taylor, Muddy Waters, Howlin' Wolf, Etta James, Janis Joplin, Bessie Smith, Robert Johnson, John Lee Hooker, Denise Lasalle, Lead Belly, B.B. King, Buddy Guy, Big Mama Thornton, Mississippi John Hurt, and Sister Rosetta Tharpe.

Later, I started enjoying jazz and listening to it every day. Some of the jazz musicians and jazz singers whom I like are John Coltrane, Miles Davis, Nina Simone, Cassandra Wilson, Sarah Vaughan, Dizzy Gillespie, Dave Brubeck, Billie Holiday, Brian Culbertson, Mindi Abair, Esperanza Spalding, Keiko Matsui, Stan Getz, Nneena Freelon, Ramsey Lewis, Ella Fitzgerald, Louis Armstrong, Cannonball Adderley, Duke Ellington, Thelonious Monk, Nancy Wilson, Lionel Hampton, Chet Baker, Sade, Youn Sun Nah, and Lester Young, among others.

Before the pandemic and lockdown, I sang in two choirs at church. Some of my favorite gospel singers are the Williams Brothers, Rev. Luther Barnes, Pastor Shirley Caesar, Andrae Crouch, Mighty Clouds of Joy, Canton Spirituals, CeCe Winans, BeBe Winans, Nashville Life Music, Donald Lawrence, Koryn Hawthorne, Kirk Franklin, Rance Allen, Tasha Cobbs Leonard, Hezekiah Walker, William McDowell, Bishop Paul S. Morton and the FGBCF Mass Choir, Yolanda Adams, Marvin Sapp, Tamela Mann, Donnie

McClurkin, Mary Mary, Tramaine Hawkins, Rev. James Cleveland, Mahalia Jackson, and Rev. F. C. Barnes and Rev. Janice Brown, among others.

For more than two decades, I performed my poetry with jazz musicians and jazz bands. During the lockdown, I played gospel songs daily and sang along with them. To that end, I knew I wanted to incorporate music into my poetry. When writing poetry, I can feel the rhythm within each line. I think the poem leads me in various musical directions. The topic or subject also leads me in certain musical directions. Music references are incorporated in many of my poems, as you have noted.

LS: In your use of music, and in your incorporation of other touchstones—reference points, stylistic features, social and political stances—both the African diaspora and African American history, literature, and culture are very strong presences in your poems. I'm thinking, for example, of your poems "Yoruba" and "Interrogation of Harriet Tubman." Some of these poems are quite musical and lyrical, such as "Yoruba," while others, such as "Tubman," fall into several categories and styles, such as the persona poem and narrative lyrics driven by a strong storytelling motive.

LDM: I'm honored and humbled by your close reading of my poetry and noting what touchstones are incorporated into my poetry. I definitely include African American history and culture in my poetry. Then, too, literature does have a presence in my poetry. I'm delighted that you have noted my poems "Yoruba" and "Interrogation of Harriet Tubman," among others falling into several traditions. I have read Langston Hughes and Gwendolyn Brooks again and again. They both incorporate African American history and culture into their poetry. With my reading of them, I feel they are literary mentors. When I was growing up, my grandfather told fascinating stories. He was a great storyteller. To that end, I have always been drawn to storytelling. I wanted to document through lyric and narrative. I believe that the poet can develop characters through the persona poem and narrative lyrics. Hopefully, the poet's voice resonates through those techniques. I hope the poems are memorable.

I think it is the poet's job to incorporate social and political subjects into his or her poetry. To that end, I think the poet does take a stance with his or her poetry. Can one write without purpose? I don't think so. When one writes nature poetry, he or she still takes a stance. Maybe poets can help to keep trees growing in the forest without being cut down. Like people planting trees on Arbor Day, maybe poets can lead the public to plant trees, too. Thus, it is important to write about those things that shock, sting, and stun. If the poet works hard enough on his or her poetry, then he or she can still infuse music into his or her poetry. At least, I hope I can work on my poetry until it sings.

LS: As a follow-up to the last question, family histories and connections also seem to motivate many of your poems, such as "Stitches." A painful subject, for which I have tremendous empathy, is the passing of your dear daughter, Maiisha L. Moore, who was also a talented poet. A poem like "Reminiscing Daddy" is exquisite in its suffering and combines the surreal with a dreamscape. Could you please discuss the role of the family in your poems, and if you wish, it would be helpful if you could please discuss how various family members have inspired and influenced your use of different poetic forms, styles, and purposes—perhaps even broadened your poetic range?

LDM: Yes, family histories and connections have motivated many of my poems. For example, *Forever Home* has several such poems in it. Decades ago, I completed a manuscript about my grandfather and grandmother, employing the tanka form. During the spring 1992 semester, I wrote a series of poems about my father's Vietnam experience, including the return home. I have also written several poems about the loss of my daughter. When writing about my daughter, I employed more than twenty-five different poetic forms. I challenged myself to write with so many different poetic forms. I went to the library daily, sat in a quiet room, and taught myself to write in various poetic forms. Some of them were difficult, but I continued to work on my craft.

Now I write poetry in more than thirty different poetic forms. Haiku is my dominant form for writing. Regarding some of my poems about family members, my mother has asked me to write poems for kinfolks' funerals, such as my grandmother, my great-aunts, my aunt, and my father. My sister asked me to write a poem for my brother-in-law's funeral. In addition, I have written poems for celebrations, such as birthdays and weddings; I have written several wedding poems. One of the wedding poems was for my former college student's wedding. When my great-great-aunt turned one hundred, I wrote a traditional poem and read it at her birthday celebration, which was held at our hometown church.

Moreover, I have written a poem for a state superintendent's retirement celebration and another for a former Miss North Carolina, who was celebrated at a program at the North Carolina Department of Public Instruction. My pastor has asked me to write poems for Mother's Day celebrations. One of the former college campus presidents invited me to write a poem for his inauguration. To that end, I read the poem on the program at the college campus inauguration for the new president. I have written poems or lyrics for performances with jazz musicians and jazz bands.

LS: Some of your poems combine several of the elements I've noted above—music, African American history, portraits, persona poems, and specific references to poets and writers who have influenced you. An example is "Bop: Coaching Poets."

LDM: Yes, I have written several poems about poets and writers who have influenced me. Of course, I have written poems about Langston Hughes, Gwendolyn Brooks, and my poetry professor Gerald Barrax. I have also written poems about or dedicated to my poetry mentors Jerry W. Ward Jr. and Eugene B. Redmond. I have also written poems about or dedicated to A. R. Ammons, Fred Chappell, Rita Dove, Michael S. Harper, Nikki Giovanni, Elizabeth Alexander, Cornelius Eady, Toi Derricotte, Angela Jackson, Natasha Trethewey, Bob Kaufman, Gary Snyder, Amiri Baraka, Sonia Sanchez, Elizabeth Searle Lamb, and others.

In addition, I have written poems about or dedicated to several members of the Carolina African American Writers' Collective. Moreover, I have written poems about or dedicated to some members of Cave Canem. In my poem, "Bop: Coaching Poets," I have referenced Quincy Troupe and Yusef Komunyakaa. When some of my students, who were women athletes, told me in class that some of the male athletes wrote poetry but didn't want it known, I was compelled to write a poem. I thought that there might be other male athletes, thinking the same thing would be true at other college campuses. To that end, I had hoped my poem would have universal appeal. I must say that I also incorporate other elements, which we have not discussed. For example, I have incorporated biblical references into *A Temple Looming*. There are biblical names incorporated into some of the poems.

LS: I'd like to return to the fact that you have written vast quantities of poems in what might be described as two different modes: there are your better-known poems in haiku and other forms associated with Asian traditions and your perhaps less well-known poems in many varied forms, including free verse, which come out of the Anglo-American or Eurocentric tradition. Do you view these as separate or connected bodies of writing? How are they complementary, and how do they differ? Do you turn to one or the other tradition when you wish to write about specific themes, experiences, memories, or emotions?

LDM: I think my poems in the varied Western forms are more expansive and lend themselves to more musical tones. However, I like the power of haiku in its conciseness and precision. For me, several of the Western forms are more challenging, such as villanelle, sestina, syllabics, prose poems, rondel, triolet, dramatic monologues, kwansabas, etcetera. Haiku, however, has enabled me to hone my poetry writing in other poetic forms. I have tried to incorporate various themes into my haiku writing, though maybe symbolically and through allusions. I am selective with diction while trying to incorporate musical elements into my haiku writing. I think voice establishes itself over time, especially when one becomes more certain of himself or herself with the poetry writing. To that end, I feel that I know what I am attempting to do with my haiku writing and intention. I hope all of my poems are complementary to one another, though some must be divergent, due to experimentation. I think the forms and structures serve my aesthetic purposes because they allow the space for possibilities and discovery. I do not know where various poetic forms will lead me within my poetry writing. I like that sense of discovery when writing.

I would like to revisit your question about structure because I certainly employ structure in all my poetry. For example, I employ couplets in some poems; tercets in some poems; and quatrains in some poems. There are times when I employ five-line stanzas or six-line stanzas in my poems. Most times I try to keep the same number of lines in each stanza throughout my poems so that I can create symmetry in my poetry. Many of my poems consist of a single stanza or one long stanza. When writing, I go wherever the poem leads me. At times, the literary elements lead me in certain directions. For example, if I employ end rhyme, then I usually know what the rhyme scheme will be for the poem. If I employ internal rhyme, then I know how the line might sound. At times, I employ slant rhyme, too. In many of my jazz poems, I employ repetition, riffs, improvisation, modulation, onomatopoeia, assonance, and consonance. There are times when I employ euphony, too. More importantly, I employ allusions and symbols in my jazz poetry. It depends upon the type of poem I might write. I strive to effectively employ enjambment and end-stopped lines. Blues poems, for example, have a particular structure.

LS: This is very helpful. Could you please elaborate on your poetic process in more detail? How do you see the balance between seeking to establish continuity, patterns, and symmetry in your poetic practice while also seeking discovery, surprise, and change? Perhaps you might wish to discuss your use of poetic techniques and devices that engender a sustained practice but also allow for progress and growth.

LDM: When I write poetry, my first draft is not always similar to my final draft. I guess I keep writing until I find the poetry because I try to incorporate texture into my poetry. By texture, I mean that I constantly try to employ as many literary elements in my poetry as possible, such as history, culture, etcetera. Naming in my poetry is also very important to me. In short, I write toward specificity in my poetry. For example, I tell my students I cannot see a bird, but I can see a robin, blue jay, cardinal, etcetera. I also tell them that I cannot see a tree, but I can see an elm, oak, ash tree, etcetera. I name places in my poetry, too. However, I delete or cross out unnecessary words in my revision process.

I look forward to finding connections with metaphors and similes. At times, I look for parallels. There are times when I employ anaphora in my poetry. There also are times when I want to incorporate particular words into my poems. Then, too, there are times when I want to incorporate variations of words into my poems. Yet, there are times when I employ an extended metaphor or motif. There is discovery in poetry writing. I love writing letter poems or epistolary poems.

Thus, I don't always know where the poem is going. I simply go in the direction that the poem takes me, though there are times when I have an idea of where the poem wants to go. In short, I write until the poem can't be written any other way. I must be able to let the poem go.

LS: Your response opens a window into your personal employment of poetic techniques and how they relate to your aesthetic goals. It also illuminates how these practices relate to your teaching methods. That's very helpful since you are renowned as a teacher, both in the context of the Carolina African American Writers' Collective and your university teaching. Would you please continue to explain your poetic techniques and purposes by relating them to specific poems as examples?

LDM: "Swinging Cool," "Raleigh Jazz Festival, 1986," "Sunday Evening," and "At the Train Stop" are a few of the several jazz poems that are included in *The Geography of Jazz*. "A Reminiscing Daddy" and "Bop: Coaching Poets" are bops, which is a poetic form that Afaa Michael Weaver invented at Cave Canem. Like my poem "Interrogation of Harriet Tubman," "Ascension: John Coltrane" is a persona poem. *Desert Storm: A Brief History* is one long poem, employing a series of haiku or a haiku sequence. *Long Rain* consists of tanka and haibun. A few years ago, an interview with me was conducted by John Zheng, and several of my poems were featured in *Valley Voices*. My poems consist of several different poetic forms, such as blues poem, jazz poem, sestina, ekphrastic, etcetera. One of my ghazals also was published in that issue of the journal. I have a blank verse poem in *A Temple Looming*. I hope my readers will notice the poems or look them up for greater insight into my poetry.

LS: You have radically redesigned and repurposed conventional forms, and such transformations reflect the impulses of modernist precursors. That includes Ezra Pound's dictum to "make it new" and William Carlos Williams's use of the line to engender dynamic movement and shared aesthetic values and practices with objectivism and imagism. Would you please offer some further comments and elaboration on how you have been influenced by modernist poets and their patterns of experimentation, innovation, exploration, and discovery by means of the poem? Since several modernist poets such as Pound also were strongly influenced by Asian forms and culture, perhaps you might also wish to comment on whether the spirit of experimentation is an area where Asian and Anglo-American forms align for you.

LDM: I have read, studied, and taught William Carlos Williams, Ezra Pound, Wallace Stevens, and Amy Lowell. So, I am aware of the imagism movement because I taught the imagism-movement poets decades ago. I have often taught Williams's poem "The Red Wheelbarrow." I have also often taught Pound's poem "In a Station of the Metro." I have taught Stevens's poem "Anecdote of the Jar." And I have taught Amy Lowell's poem "The Pond." Her poem makes me think about Matsuo Bashō's famous "old pond" haiku. I have heard of the objectivism movement, including George Oppen. Many poets have been influenced by William Carlos Williams, including me. My poem "Twenty-Six Views of Christmas" is a long poem, consisting of a series of tanka or a tanka sequence. I have written many haiku sequences. I have also experimented with the haiku form. For example, I have written jazzku, bluesku, and gospelku. I have also experimented with haiku and tanka until I wrote "American Jazzku," which was published in *The Geography of Jazz*. Haiku writing leads the poet to pay attention to close detail. I think the more I experiment with haiku, the more elements I incorporate into the poem. For example, decades ago, I informed a poet-friend that I incorporate three of the sensory perceptions into my haiku rather than just two of them. At that time, I noticed that many haiku poets incorporated two of the sensory perceptions. Later I found out he had written an essay about my experimenting with three sensory perceptions. I think that is all I will say about the form at this time. Maybe I'll write my own article about my experimenting with three sensory perceptions in the future, regarding my haiku. I am grateful to you for such a great question. I prefer to write the poem and let others examine my poetry, though I do often employ present tense. As you can see, it is not wise to discuss projects with which one might be engaged.

LS: The presence of women is quite prominent in *A Temple Looming*, and I'm thinking especially of part 2, which is exclusively focused on photographic representations of women. Relatedly, many of these poems are what could be described as portraiture. This is an area where I see differences in what you produce in (relatively speaking) longer forms compared to haiku and the traditional dimensions (which clearly you know and respect) of how haiku operates. I also note that many of these descriptive poems interject the perspective of the "I" who is observing and even expressing wishes about and for these women. Do you care to comment on the role and importance of women in your poems?

LDM: I wanted to somehow get to know the women in the photographs that triggered the poems. To that end, I tried to imagine their stories. Of course, I researched the era, too. But I spent a lot of time with my aunts, great aunts, mother, grandmother, great-grandmother, and great-great-aunt. Thus, I think those visitations allowed me insight into my poetry writing for *A Temple Looming*. At least, I hope so. In fact, I hope I have probed deeper into the women's lives inhabiting my poems. I have read, studied, and taught many women poets' poetry in my classes, workshops, and seminars. Some of the several women poets whom I have studied are Julia Alvarez, Maya Angelou, Cathy Smith Bowers, Gwendolyn Brooks, Kelly Cherry, Allison Adelle Hedge Coke, Rita Dove, Camille Dungy, Nikki Giovanni, Kimiko Hahn, Linda Hogan, Sharon Olds, Anne Sexton, Emily Dickinson, Elizabeth Bishop, Lucille Clifton, Anna Akhmatova, Kendra Hamilton, Marianne Moore, Mary Oliver, Adrienne Rich, Sylvia Plath, Sonia Sanchez, Evie Shockley, Marilyn Nelson, Patricia Smith, Margaret Walker, and Phillis Wheatley. I wanted to write beyond mere descriptions because the photographs have already done so. I also wanted to challenge myself to write, hopefully effectively, about women.

LS: This is quite helpful. As I view it, women play a significant role in what we are regarding as your "Western tradition" poems. What is the precise relationship between your view of women and your poetics? Do you perhaps view women as "muses," "guiding spirits," or inspirational forces, in a sense? Do you care to comment on any social or human rights movements of the past or present where women have played a major part?

LDM: Yes, women muses certainly guide some of my poems. Women have played a large role in my life. For example, my brothers, cousins, and I worked with our great-grandmother in her peanut fields and cornfields. She cooked great meals for us. I watched her make quilts in her living room. We sat on the porch with her, talking and laughing. I worked in my grandmother's chicken coop, gathering eggs. I watched my grandmother make biscuits. I taught poetry workshops to senior citizens for my grandmother's Friendly Blue Light organization. My great-grandmother and great aunt taught me gardening. Our mother taught my brothers, sisters, and me how to cook. I watched our mother sew. She made me a black-and-white tuxedo. I also watched our mother make hats and other arts and crafts. When I was growing up, I viewed her artwork. She drew beautiful works of art. I watched my aunt braid hair. I also watched her cook. She also prepared meals at my grandmother's house. Many of those observations and experiences have triggered poems for me. I have written several poems that were inspired by the Black arts movement women poets, writers, and artists, especially Sonia Sanchez, Nikki Giovanni, Angela Jackson, Ntozake Shange, Mari Evans, June Jordan, and Carolyn Rodgers. Going beyond the question of women specifically and commenting on my political poetry, in 2020, I wrote a series of poems about George Floyd and/or poems dedicated to him. During the past few decades, I have written poems dedicated to Rodney King, Trayvon Martin, Elizabeth Keckley, Zora Neale Hurston, Alice Walker, and Richard Wright, among others.

LS: Thank you for such a beautiful and illuminating answer, which presents vivid details about important women who inspired some of your most prominent poetic themes and values. Some of your poems which I view as still life or formal portraiture, both of men and women, combine static description with a great deal of hidden, interior action. In other words, the images are of surfaces, and yet the poet uses the evocation of these surfaces to reveal character, personality, history, and even relationships with the first-person-speaking subject, the "I" persona, as I mentioned. I see the influence of William Carlos Williams in these poems, some of which are ekphrastic, evoking both paintings and photographs. You create mental pictures through the visual description, and a strong sense of motion through your largely enjambed line breaks. Would you like to discuss the relationship between visual observation and language in your poems? Perhaps you might also comment on some poets (and/or artists) whose work has influenced you as you've polished your tremendous observational skills.

LDM: Yes, I have read and studied William Carlos Williams's poetry. I have also learned about enjambment from my former poetry professor Gerald Barrax and from Miller Williams, who wrote lots of dramatic monologues. My professor often discussed incorporating the right word or exact word into our poetry in class. I think such teaching has something to do with the language in my poems. Haiku has taught me much about visual observation. The need to incorporate vivid imagery has also enabled me to sharpen visual observation. As you pointed out, I have written ekphrastic poems, but I did not know that term at the time of composition. Thus, I was not aware that I had written ekphrastic poems because the term was not popular decades ago. I simply wrote poems about old photographs, paintings, and other forms of art and culture, including . . . music, woodworking, glass blowing, blacksmithing, and dance. I have also written several poems about sports. I used to attend basketball games, softball games, soccer, and track-and-field meets on campus and write poems about those events. The chaplain invited me to read poems in the campus chapel, including my basketball poems.

In addition, I collaborated with colleagues in the Visual Art Department and Music Department. For example, we created the Satire Project, which consists of paintings, poetry, and music. There is a CD and a book for the Satire Project. Then there was a collaboration with another colleague. I wrote poems inspired by her paintings and photography. She had an exhibition which featured her artwork and my poetry. I read my poetry at her opening art exhibition. Decades ago, the Carolina African American Writers' Collective collaborated with various artists, such as a photographer, a printmaker, and a sculptor. I have also collaborated with choreographers. I have written several renga, renku, and rengay with other poets. For example, I have written renga with Ruth Yarrow, Gerald C. Little, Lorraine Ellis Harr, Elizabeth Searle Lamb, and Virginia Brady Young, among many others. I have written renku with Francine Porad, Fay Aoyagi, Debra Kang Dean, and several others. I have written rengay with Garry Gay, Michael Dylan Welch, Alice Frampton, Crystal Simone Smith, Kathleen O'Toole, and others. I have participated in renku sessions in Japan, Canada, and throughout the United States. I have participated in William J. Higginson's renku sessions in the United States, Marsha Hryciuk's renku sessions in Canada, and Tadashi Kondo's renku sessions in Japan. I have also participated in several other poets' renku sessions, including Patricia J. Machmiller. I have written tan-renga with Dave Russo. I like the sense of discovery that collaborations might initiate.

LS: May we please discuss the role of lineation in your poetry? Have the compressions and motion of the haiku form impacted your use of line breaks in poems that are not haiku? What other factors enter your decisions on lineation, stanzaic structure, and use of forms?

LDM: Yes, haiku has certainly impacted my use of line breaks in my poems. I have also written syllabic poetry. In addition, musical elements have impacted my use of line breaks in my poems. Moreover, the various poetic forms have also impacted my use of line breaks in my poems. In short, it depends upon my poetic aim or poetic purpose regarding the use of line breaks in my poems. I am constantly trying to do something new or original within my poetry. I am attentive to my line breaks because I believe the lines should end with strong words. For example, I don't usually end a line with a preposition. If I am writing syllabics, then the line might lend itself to such an ending. When writing haiku, I believe that every line is important. Thus, I work with my haiku until I feel the poem is ready to speak or sing. I hope my poems are memorable. Originality is extremely important to me. For that reason, it is important to read very widely to know what has already been written. I try to write the best poem I possibly can with the poetic tools in my toolbox. What no one can teach is experience. My experience informs my poetry. Observation also informs my poetry. There is no one thing that leads me to write poetry. I hope my poetry is multilayered.

LS: I note a strong sense of place and rootedness in your writing, as well as a deep awareness of family, lineage, legacy, and racial history. Here I'm thinking of several poems in part 3 of *A Temple Looming.* Please discuss the role of both geographical place and African American history (past and present, personal and universal) in your poems and how location and experience may be interconnected. I'm happy for you to take this (and any) question in whatever direction you wish.

LDM: I am delighted to know that you have noticed that a strong sense of place emerges from my writing. I have always felt a kinship to the land, especially because I have done lots of farm work, gardening, and listening to the stories of older kinfolks. So, yes, I often incorporate family, lineage, legacy, and racial history into my poetry. I try to do the same thing with my haiku writing, if possible. I want to write poems that are necessary and, hopefully, that resonate. I am grateful to you for such thought-provoking questions. Geography and African American history are evident in my poetry because of my experience. I have documented my experience in America, particularly the American South. I have traveled to other countries, such as Germany, Mexico, Canada, the Bahamas, and Japan. I have written poetry in all those places. No matter where I travel, I return home somehow in my writing from time to time. I find that the greater distance I am from home, then I miss it more. Therefore, I am able to write about place, ancestral memory, family, and storytelling. Racial history has entered many of my poems because I think it is important to acknowledge and remember. I hope my readers are able to glean deeper meanings from my poetry.

In fact, I hope my readers will experience a multiplicity of meanings from my poetry. I have written many poems about my decades of gardening. I think gardening is similar to poetry writing in some ways, such as exploration, imagination, and concentration. For examples of my gardening and family, please read *Forever Home*. Many of the poems in the book are free verse, though there are traditional poems, too. I hope the different types of poems reveal my range. I also hope my readers will get a sense of my voice through my books. In addition, I hope my poems say something about me as a human being. What does it mean to be a poet? I want my poetry to be able to provide some insight into what it means to be a poet. We, as poets, have a responsibility to our readers. And that responsibility is to tell our truths.

LS: As our interview draws to a close, what kind of response do you hope for from your readers? And how do you view the role of the poet and poetry in the world today?

LDM: I think the role of poetry is to document the world in which we live and bring about change and healing. For example, I have been writing ecopoetry for several decades. In fact, I wrote ecopoetry long before the term became popular. I have also written about grief through my poetry. What about aging, health, class, and race? Poetry can effectively provide insight into all those topics. Let's keep writing and documenting through our perspectives. We need everyone's story to create a quilt of living books that contain a wealth of multiethnic and multiracial experiences. Then we will have the American Story as it should be. I will keep telling my story and working towards a multiplicity of meanings in my poetry. I long to write poetry that is memorable. Like a carpenter, I will build poems frame by frame. To that end, I will keep experimenting with various building materials or literary elements. Thank you very much for such a deep interior interview.

Jazz Poetry as a Message of African American Culture: An Interview with Lenard D. Moore

John Zheng / 2023

From *Mississippi Quarterly* 75, no. 1 (2023): 99–110. Reprinted by permission.

Based in Raleigh, North Carolina, Lenard D. Moore is a prolific poet with seven poetry collections. Known internationally as a haiku poet, Moore shows his great interest in various poetic forms and expressions in *The Geography of Jazz*, published by Mountains and Rivers Press in 2018 and reprinted by Blair in September 2020, which brings us his jazz experience and feeling. To Moore, jazz is a celebration of American life and culture. This celebration challenges him to present such great jazz musicians as Max Roach, John Coltrane, Thelonious Monk, Duke Ellington, Ray Charles, or the unknown ones described in the poem "Raleigh Jazz Festival, 1986." The impact is immediate as *The Geography of Jazz* renews the jazz performances. This interview, conducted by email in February and October 2021 and revised in March 2022, serves as a complement to a previous interview, conducted in 2017, which focused mainly on Moore's haiku writing and other books.

John Zheng: How important is jazz as an essential musical expression of African American experience?

Lenard D. Moore: Jazz is one of the great musical genres, which African Americans invented in New Orleans around one hundred twenty-one years ago or around the turn of the last century, the twentieth century. An expressive form, it is so important that it emerges in the way we talk and walk.

JZ: And how important is it to American culture?

LDM: Jazz is vital to American culture because it is part of the fabric and part of the quilt of America. It is appreciated and celebrated all over the world. To that end, America is jazz as well as other forms of music. Jazz has a way of bringing everyone together. When we come together, love happens.

JZ: What has urged you to write jazz poetry?

LDM: It is the feel of jazz and the improvisation that have led me to write jazz poetry. I also like what Langston Hughes, Michael S. Harper, Amiri Baraka, Sonia Sanchez, Jayne Cortez, Yusef Komunyakaa, and Eugene B. Redmond have done with jazz poetry. In fact, Harper's book, *Dear John, Dear Coltrane*, has been such an important book to me. I reread Harper's book again and again. He incorporated much history as well as music into his poetry. I like his approach to writing jazz poetry. I, too, employ history in my poetry. I want to capture the mood and innovation of jazz and infuse it into my poetry.

In addition, I like to take risks with my poetry writing. I do not want to be pigeonholed with my poetry. I keep doing new things. I write poetry in more than thirty different poetic forms. I think experimentation has a way of bringing about discovery. So, maybe I am able to work toward a sense of discovery in my jazz poetry by pushing the boundaries or extending the boundaries. If possible, I strive to write until the jazz poem sings back at me.

JZ: Poetry is a carrier of music. Is there an emphasis on the title of your poetry collection *The Geography of Jazz*?

LDM: Yes, there is a definite emphasis on the title of my poetry collection. My original manuscript was cut about thirty pages because I wrote about jazz artists and jazz tunes from all over the world. I really had a focus on the geography of jazz. So, I came up with the title of my manuscript several years ago. I worked on my manuscript for more than twenty years. At some point, however, I hope to publish the other section of my original manuscript. My original manuscript depicts jazz musicians and singers from Japan, South Korea, South Africa, Brazil, and elsewhere. I like different schools of jazz, including bebop. I am interested in what newer artists are doing, such as Esperanza Spalding, Keiko Matsui, and Young Sun Nah. Of course, I love the standards or classic jazz tunes.

JZ: Who are your favorite jazz musicians who have invigorated your jazz poetry?

LDM: Musicians who have invigorated my jazz poetry are John Coltrane, Miles Davis, Nina Simone, Dizzy Gillespie, Thelonious Monk, Cassandra Wilson, Oliver Lake, Ramsey Lewis, and Duke Ellington. I like Dave Brubeck's, Stan Getz's, and Keiko Matsui's jazz tunes. For me, my go-to jazz musicians are John Coltrane and Miles Davis. I like the jazz singers Billie Holiday, Ella Fitzgerald, and Young Sun Nah. I also like newer jazz artists, such as Eliane Elias, Esperanza Spalding, Branford Marsalis, and Nneena Freelon.

JZ: What was their influence in finding your voice?

LDM: I do not know whether they had influenced me in finding my voice. I think all of my decades of writing, reading, and teaching helped me find my voice. Without a doubt, jazz has made a significant impact on my poetry. I think my book *The Geography of Jazz* signals the impact that jazz has made on my poetry. I hope my readers will also listen to jazz tunes by the artists with whom I have tried to document.

JZ: How did you transcribe your voice into lines when you wrote a jazz poem?

LDM: I think breaths, rhythm, and feeling enable me to transcribe my voice into lines. The freedom of improvisation also enables me to transcribe my voice into lines when I write a jazz poem. Ancestral memory also enables me to transcribe my voice into lines. Without my ancestors, I would not have been able to do such work.

JZ: Did you hear the lines?

LDM: Yes. I think the divine helps with further enabling me to transcribe my voice into lines when I write a jazz poem because it is a spiritual journey. I read my lines aloud.

JZ: Did you ever imagine talking with a musician when you were composing a jazz poem?

LDM: I do not know how to accomplish such a thing. I am only able to talk with jazz musicians in actuality and real time, though we might be able to feel a jazz musician's spirit hovering when we write. My concentration is reading, writing, and teaching. I will leave the analysis of my jazz poetry to literary scholars, cultural critics, American studies, and African American studies scholars. However, I do know about capturing the feel or the feeling of jazz when I write a jazz poem.

JZ: To get a sense of jazz melody and emotion, do you go to a club or juke joint to listen to live jazz or stay in your basement to listen to albums?

LDM: Yes, I most certainly listen to live jazz at festivals and concerts. In the past, I have listened to jazz in a club, in music halls, in museums, and in cultural centers. During the COVID-19 pandemic, I have not been able to listen to live jazz. I have listened to CDs, satellite jazz, and radio jazz. I have not played jazz albums in a long time, though I love listening to them in the basement.

JZ: Jazz enhances a listener's feeling, but jazz poetry challenges a reader's intellect. How do you inspire a reader to feel the rhythm of your poetry?

LDM: I employed several literary elements, such as alliteration, assonance, repetition, onomatopoeia, rhythm, enjambment, end-stopped lines, and variation. I know there are other literary elements, which I employ. Yet, I certainly employ auditory imagery when I write a jazz poem.

JZ: "Swinging Cool" is a poem that requires an oral reading to get the flavor of jazz rhythm:

"Swinging Cool"

The bassist hugs
the bass, plunks it.
Ting, boom, ting boom—
the drummer beats
and booms. Saxophonist
weaves notes, oscillates, blows
and the pianist finger-dances
on the keys: "Swinging
at the Haven." Musicians spark
the sheet music stands
and angled microphones.
Blue backdrop.
Modulating that tempo,
they work the tune.
Drumsticks knocking time,
piano plucking our ears.
Bassman still hugging
the bass, straight sets—
walls thrumming—
steady as the spring moon
inciting the indigo sky.

Can you talk about it to help us experience jazz through your language? How did you swing the music into this poem? Or what was your creative process? Your craft of writing this poem will be interesting to know.

LDM: I think the image of the jazz band triggered the poem, but when the musicians began playing, the feel of the music took over the moment. I also think my decades of haiku writing at once guided my longhand writing of the poem. Then various literary elements came into play, such as assonance, onomatopoeia, repetition, alliteration, allusion, and imagery.

I wanted to employ strong verbs. For example, "hugs," "plunks," "beats," "booms," "weaves," "oscillates," "blows," "finger-dances," "spark," and "work" are all active verbs. All the verbs conjure an image or picture, except for "work." The third line, which is italicized, highlights the onomatopoeia. I use particular nouns to enhance specificity and details in the poem. I use the "ing" words or gerunds to enhance the continuous motion or movement in the poem. I use "haven" for a sense of safety and hopefully as a tribute to the Harlem Renaissance. The poem opens with four syllables in each of the first four lines. Then the fifth line has six syllables, and so forth. All those elements and/or strategies contribute to the shaping of the poem. I think the shaping of the poem also helps with the music. I wrote the poem at an indoor concert. I glanced at the spring moon through an upper window in the music hall on campus. I wanted to include that image in the poem. I also wanted to establish the mood within the poem. At the same time, I wanted to somehow capture the feel of the music. In addition, I wanted my poem to be a performance like the jazz band because they were cooking and to enliven my readers' appreciation of jazz poetry.

JZ: Does your poetry intend to present a kind of experience gained from jazz performances?

LDM: I hope my poetry captures the feel of jazz performances. I also hope it somehow opens up to a spiritual, cosmic, and memorable effect.

JZ: A jazz poem with a memorable effect can touch an audience not only through reading but also through performance, just like what a musician does onstage. There can be an interaction between the performer and the audience. Can you share with us your experience of performing a poem?

LDM: Of course, it would depend upon how a poem might move my audiences and/or readers. I will say that when the poem begins to perform, then maybe it becomes a spiritual experience. I wrote "Sunday Evening" at Enloe High School in 1989 when Ramsey Lewis performed in the auditorium. His performance was all instrumental. I wrote "At the Train Stop" on a train trip to New York City. The train made a stop in Rocky Mount, Thelonious Monk's hometown. The train trip happened during autumn. I wanted to depict the season in the poem, too. I also wanted to convey feelings in my poems. Like buckets, the shapes of my poems carry the truths, the lens, and the interplay of language. For me, a jazz poem improvises and bends language. To that end, diction, syntax, and implications are vital. And yet, the persona must be trustworthy. I want to dialogue with my readers. So, I hope they will answer the question. I also hope my answer to your question is a guide to how one might understand a spiritual, cosmic, and memorable effect. In addition, I hope the reader will bring his or her own experience to my jazz poems.

JZ: Was jazz an inseparable part of your coming of age?

LDM: I listened to some jazz in my teenage years, mostly Herbie Hancock. It was in my very early twenties, from twenty to twenty-one, when I began listening to jazz daily.

JZ: So, Herbie Hancock should have held a special position in your teenage years. How did you fall in love with his music? Anything special in his voice or his expression?

LDM: At the time, the rhythm and beats in Herbie Hancock captured me. In fact, I believe it was his tune "Feet Don't Fail Me Now" that kept me attentive. The tune had such power and energy. Earlier we talked about memory; Herbie Hancock's jazz tunes are memorable. "Feet Don't Fail Me Now" certainly was one of those types of jazz tunes that makes the listener move. If you do not move, then you cannot be alive. To that end, his jazz expression compels the audience to listen, snap, sway, swing, and dance. His music invites the audience into the moment. My uncle played Herbie Hancock's album all the time, blasting it. I could hear the music as I walked up the dirt road beside our house to their house—he and my aunt. I hope my comments reveal how I fell in love with the music. I am grateful for your question that resurfaced long-ago memories, regarding my early music appreciation.

JZ: I like what you said, "if you do not move, then you cannot be alive." In reading your poem "Interlude," which functions as an intermission in as short as six lines:

> nothing but chops
> baby, yes, chops
> nothing but chops
> yes, yes, yes
> chops, nothing but
> chops, baby, yes

I feel there is a move to be rhythmically alive. Any words about the rhythm or did you intend to represent the beat of a jazz musician?

LDM: I wanted to shift the beats and hopefully evoke somewhat mellow emotions. Please note that each line, which you have quoted, consists of four syllables, except for the line with "yes" repeated three times so that the passage would not be sing-song. Yes, there is an intermission. I strove to use euphony throughout the passage because I wanted to create a softer effect. I hope that is the way the poem works for my readers and/or listeners.

JZ: Did you write about family history in your jazz poetry?

LDM: My book *Forever Home* depicts the family history, farming, and a sense of place. I do not think my jazz poetry explores much family history, though I know I must have incorporated some family history when I first began writing jazz poetry decades ago.

JZ: Jazz is an emotional message. Did you write jazz poetry to tell a powerful story of Black life and culture?

LDM: Yes, I wanted to document Black life and culture in my jazz poetry. I also wanted to explore one of the genres of music that I love and appreciate. Moreover, I wanted to depict what my people are creating. Furthermore, I wanted to demonstrate how jazz became a part of me and how I became a part of jazz. In other words, jazz is the reason I write jazz poetry. Then, of course, I read jazz poetry.

JZ: Can you give us an example? I mean, can you use a poem to demonstrate how jazz is a part of you?

LDM: Yes, I will include my poem "At the Train Stop," which is one-stanza long:

> I imagine the quick hand:
> Thelonious Monk waves
> at red, orange, yellow leaves
> from Raleigh to Rocky Mount.
> Alone in this seat,
> I peer out the half-window
> at the rainbow of faces
> bent toward this train
> that runs to the irresistible Apple,
> determine to imagine Monk
> glows like Carolina sun
> in cloudless blue sky.
> I try so hard to picture him
> until his specter hunkers
> at the ghost piano, foxfire
> on concrete platform.
> Now I can hear the tune "Misterioso"
> float on sunlit air.
> If notes were visible,

perhaps they would drift crimson,
shimmer like autumn leaves.
A hunch shudders
into evening, a wordless flight.

JZ: My favorite poem is "Max Roach Speaks to an Audiophile." I can hear the drumbeats. What was your creative process for writing it?

LDM: I have listened to Max Roach play drums. He played incredible drum rolls. He also was born in North Carolina. Several of the renowned jazz musicians and singers are from North Carolina. I, too, am from North Carolina. Most importantly, I wanted to write about them because of the effectiveness of their jazz tunes.

JZ: How did you add creativity to your jazz poetry?

LDM: I read and study poetry. To that end, I wanted to take risks and try to innovate my jazz poetry. Maybe this is the reason why I wrote, revised, and tweaked my manuscript for two decades or more. I wanted to work on it until I got it right. The precision of decades of haiku writing has also influenced my jazz poetry. I try to infuse yugen and sabi into it, too. There are so many elements, such as allusions and symbolism, I use to add creativity to my jazz poetry so it can resonate effectively.

JZ: How do you infuse yugen and sabi?

LDM: When I write yugen as an element in my jazz poetry, which certainly is a haiku element, I am referring to mystery. For example, I think I have infused yugen into my poems "Zora Shango" and "A Note on Improvisations." When I write sabi as an element in my jazz poetry, which also certainly is a haiku element, I am referring to beauty. For example, I think I have infused sabi into "Jazz Suite" and "At the Train Stop." Maybe a music scholar will also examine my jazz poetry. I hope scholars, students, and others will read *The Geography of Jazz* and appreciate whatever they may gather from it. I am not saying that all my jazz poems infuse those haiku elements because I use a variety of elements. I also hope my readers will know my jazz poetry before they see my name.

JZ: "Jazz Suite" in *The Geography of Jazz* is a sequence of haiku. Each haiku seems to be independent in its expression. Are they each an individual haiku about jazz and arranged together later as a sequence?

LDM: No, I wrote all the haiku in "Jazz Suite" at the same time. Yes, it's a sequence. I tried to ensure that each haiku could stand alone as an individual poem. It was hard work, but I loved the revision process. And yet, some of the haiku, I hope, worked on the first draft. I usually listen to a poem's rhythm during my writing of it. In addition, I try to use specificity and vivid imagery. I am aware of using contrast, too. Moreover, I want to use allusions and good details.

JZ: A couple of stanzas in "Intermission, 1956," such as stanza 2, read like haiku, but overall, the poem is written in tercets as it has a thematic connection between the stanzas on Billie Holiday. It's also ekphrastic. Can you talk about it?

LDM: I wrote it because a childhood friend took me to the Brooklyn Museum of Art to view an exhibit. I also listened to some of Billie Holiday's tunes. Then I let my imagination guide the poem. I felt the muse hovered over me to inspire the poem. When writing the poem, I tried to step outside it and look inside it. I felt it was a way to write towards originality, so the poem would say something new, regardless of how difficult it might be to do so. At the same time, I wanted to hopefully add depth to the poem and write beyond simply observing a photograph. I did not want to write such a poem because the photograph already reveals the scene. Furthermore, I hoped the title "Intermission, 1956" would add more meaning to the poem. To write the best possible poem, I tried to establish the mood and change up the music with the phrasing. To that end, I hope short lines and tercets appeal to my readers' eyes as well as their ears. I also hope symmetry carries the poem from beginning to end.

JZ: Was it a challenge to use the language to bring out the musicality of your jazz poetry?

LDM: Yes, it was a challenge to capture the musicality. Then, it became easier for me to use the language to bring it out. The more I read and performed my jazz poetry with musicians, the easier it became for me to explore musicality. I felt I was in sync with the musicians when I read and performed my jazz poetry on stage. At times, we were able to perform without rehearsal. It was the feel of the jazz that was happening on stage.

JZ: Did you improvise at your reading like a jazz musician?

LDM: Yes, I improvised my readings because I worked with how the music made me feel and how much synchronicity might be at work. Many times, I was able to read or perform off the energy of the audience.

JZ: How did the audience respond to your performance?

LDM: At my performances, the audience claps, snaps their fingers, bobs, rocks, sways, and sometimes dances.

JZ: How do you define your passion for jazz?

LDM: My passion is spiritual and hopefully embodies grace with much gratitude. Decades ago, at North Carolina State University's DH Hill Library,

I read the poetry in the *Mississippi Writers* anthology published by the University Press of Mississippi. I was in awe of Jerry W. Ward Jr.'s poem "Jazz to Jackson to John." It was the music in the poem that struck me. It demonstrated musical possibilities in a jazz poem. Ward also knows how to work language and make it work for the poem. I go back to that poem from time to time. I must mention Al Young. His poetry, too, was a musical influence on my jazz poetry. Young knows how to make the language turn back and bend. I am talking about pure music here. There is no way a poet can mention all the musical influences on his or her poetry.

JZ: Is your passion still burning expressively?

LDM: My passion for jazz enhances the way I express my attentiveness to craft while combining poetry with music. At some point, the poet must fly on his or her own wings. Now I spread my own wings. Let me fly with my poetic voice. I hope my readers can hear the jazz sounds. I also hope my readers can experience jazz in my poetry. In addition, I hope they return to my poetry again and again.

JZ: My last question. "Lovebeat" is a poem that presents your passion not only for jazz but for love as well. It's erotic; it's interaction; it's spiritual; it's call and response:

> My eyes like blinds
> I pull shut in her bedroom
> as she draws me close enough
> to stroke my lips.
> "Take me," she nods
> as if pulling notes
> from Miles's horn.
> Coltrane's music is gentle,
> rain quenching jazzbuds open.

How did you juxtapose the note of love and the beat of jazz? In other words, how did you imagine making jazz and love creatively into opening buds quenched by rain? Did you use Miles and Coltrane as a contrast?

LDM: I am delighted to know that you have noticed what kind of response I had hoped for from my readers, regarding "Lovebeat." So, yes, the poem presents my passion for jazz and love at the same time. I tried to create a memorable title, so I combined the words *love* and *beat* to make the speaker crave the moment. There is also the coined word *jazzbuds*. I worked on the poem for several years. I kept tweaking it until I was satisfied with its rhythm and clarity. Yes, I used Coltrane and Miles as a contrast. I also used them as allusions. I wanted the poem to work as a bridge between love and jazz. Then, too, I wanted love and jazz to converge like a river. I think the poem's progression and my years of listening to jazz guided me toward the juxtaposition of the note of love and the beat of jazz. I also think that the poem's rhythm contributed to the effect, too. I hope the words *rain* and *open* give the poem an element of sensuality and enhance symbolic meaning and literal meaning. In addition, I hope both words help to establish the mood. Thank you very much for such an undeniable thought-provoking interview.

Between Grief and the Gospel: The Poetry of Lenard D. Moore

Ce Rosenow / 2023

From *Southern Quarterly* 59, no. 1 (2024). Reprinted by permission.

Ce Rosenow: What role did religion play in your upbringing?

Lenard D. Moore: Religion was very important in my upbringing and played a major role because it helped to keep me focused on trying to do the right thing. It also enabled me to be attuned to the divine. Moreover, religion was key in advancing my study of it. Furthermore, religion empowered me by listening to the rhythm of the pastor's sermons. Religion was also empowering me to witness so many kinfolks engaged with it. For example, my great-grandmother always attended Sunday service. My great-great-aunt and several cousins also always attended Sunday service. My grandmother and my great-uncle sang in the choir. My great-aunt played the piano and ushered. My grandmother, great-uncle, and great-aunt were siblings. My sisters sang in the choir. Some of my cousins ushered and sang in the choir. After discharging from the military, I ushered. My mother has been ushering for decades. My aunts have also ushered for decades. One of them still ushers. My uncle has been ushering for decades, too. He still ushers. Another older relative has played the piano, too. One of my brothers sang in the choir, too. Another one of my brothers sang at various events. My mother sometimes sang at Usher's anniversaries, etcetera. My father could sing, too. He participated in plays at church. He also was a trustee. In short, my family has always been involved in Sunday service and other services, such as Bible study. It is not surprising that I have written poems about Sunday service, Easter service, etcetera. We were usually at Sunday service and sometimes Evening service during my upbringing.

CR: What role does religion play in your life now?

LDM: Before the pandemic lockdown, I sang in two choirs. When the state opens again fully, I plan to continue singing in the choirs. I also participated in Bible study. In addition, I attended Sunday service frequently. At times, we sang at other churches and at homecomings and funerals.

CR: What is the relationship for you personally between spirituality and creativity?

LDM: I feel my poetry embodies spirituality. Spirituality intertwines with my creativity. I hope spirituality is part of my being. I also hope gratitude, love, and grace emerge from my poetry.

CR: To what extent do your religious community and your poetry community overlap?

LDM: I think my religious community and poetry community overlap by providing a safe place for worshipping and fellowshipping. I have the freedom to worship and the freedom to experience poetry—the emotional appeal of it and the spiritual realm of it. In short, I can engage poetry without worrying about anything. In fact, poetry is a balm; it is healing without disturbance. Poetry is the safest food I can consume. In my religious community and poetry community, I am able to write beyond boundaries. In short, I am able to write poetry without having to explain my work. For example, there have been times when I have had to explain cultural references in my poetry, especially in poetry classes. I want to write poetry and concentrate on infusing music into it. There also was a time when I had to explain something to other members of the Washington Street Writers Group. The other African American member in the writers group also explained the concept of the kitchen with which I employed in my poetry, regarding African American hair.

CR: Do some of the same people participate in your religious community and your poetry community?

LDM: Yes, some of the same people participate in my religious community and my poetry community. Some of them have attended my poetry events at bookstores, libraries, museums, especially when I perform my poetry accompanied by jazz bands or jazz musicians.

I am often invited to read my poetry during Black History Month and Mother's Day celebrations in my religious community. I have also seen some of the same people from my poetry community within my religious community, too. One of the poets, who is featured in *All the Songs We Sing*, has often been in my religious community. Another person from my religious community has attended several events in my poetry community and has helped to sell my poetry books during events at libraries and bookstores. My pastor infuses some poetic elements in his sermons. He also has attended a major African American Cultural Arts Celebration, which featured the Carolina African American Writers' Collective.

CR: Do you have a favorite poem (or poems) of your own that addresses religion?

LDM: No, I do not really have a favorite poem of mine that addresses religion because I like all my poems. I cannot choose between my poems because it is like choosing between one's children. In short, my poems are my children. I treat all of my poems the same. However, I like my poem "I'm Listening to Gospel Music." I also like my haiku "Easter sermon" and "another gospel song" and "choir practice" as well as my tanka "as gospel music plays" that address religion. Several years ago, I had a longer gospel poem published in the newspaper. I feel that these poems stand out to me as examples of my poems that address religion because "I'm Listening to Gospel Music" was inspired by actually listening to an abundance of gospel music and singing along with the songs. I hope that I was able to employ a level of spirituality into my poems. I wrote my haiku "Easter sermon" at Easter service. The pastor has a way of captivating the congregation with his rhythmic delivery of any sermon as he preaches and teaches. In short, I experienced the spiritual moments and tried to write beyond the surface of them. I hope my poems address religion in such a way that my readers can experience them deeply.

CR: You have said in other interviews that you listen to gospel music almost every day. Which gospel songs are among your favorites?

LDM: Yes, I have a long list of gospel songs that I really like because there is no way that I can only have a couple of songs as my favorite gospel songs. There are times when I listen to gospel songs for hours. I usually sang along with the gospel songs. Some of my favorite gospel songs are "Still Here," "I'm Just a Nobody," "God's Grace," "My God," "Amazing Grace," "Take Me to the King," "Change Me," "Touch from You," "Every Praise," "Won't He Do It," "Deliver Me (This Is My Exodus)," and "Rough Side of the Mountain." These songs are some of my favorites because they tell stories of healing and overcoming. All of the songs express God's grace and mercy and/or supreme love and His goodness. The lyrics are memorable and embody a depth of feelings. The rhythms of the songs and their meanings are important to me. I get recharged from listening to my favorite gospel songs. For me, it is like taking my battery to get recharged so that I can run longer and stronger like my car. Somehow the gospel songs elevate my spiritual power and physical power. "God's Grace" and "Take Me to the King" are two of many songs that move me in such a way. Another aspect is the way in which the refrains might keep me singing.

CR: Who are some of your favorite gospel singers?

LDM: For me to truly try to understand gospel music, there is no way that I can have only a couple of favorite gospel singers because I try to get a feeling for voice, rhythm, lyrics, and depth of meaning. To that end, some of my favorite gospel singers are the Clark Sisters, Shirley Caesar, Marvin Sapp, the Williams Brothers, Mahaila Jackson, Luther Barnes, Tasha Cobbs Leonard, Tamela Mann, Hezekiah Walker, Koryn Hawthorne, Rev. Janice Brown, and Rev. James Cleveland and the Southern California Community Choir. Shirley Caesar and Marvin Sapp are two of the many performers whose lyrics are so meaningful. They write their own songs. They write from personal experience. They have distinct voices. Those are some of the aspects for which they are known. I play their songs again and again, each time singing along with them.

CR: You also write gospel poetry. How has gospel music impacted your gospel poems?

LDM: I think gospel music has helped with employing gospel rhythms in my gospel poems. I feel that gospel music is full of hope and love. I hope those elements are infused in my gospel poems, too.

CR: Has gospel music impacted your other poems? If so, in what ways?

LDM: Yes, I think gospel music has also impacted some of my haiku and tanka. In fact, the music impact has enabled me to hopefully infuse rhythm, tone, and emotional appeal into my other poems. I especially hope I am able to capture the feel of gospel in my other poems. Here is an example of one of my haiku, which shows the impact of gospel music:

> on the lead singer's red robe
> the microphone's shadow swaying;
> congregation claps

The above haiku was published in *Frogpond* more than thirty years ago.

CR: Have other poets' gospel poems impacted your approach to writing gospel poetry?

LDM: No, I do not think other poets' gospel poems have impacted my approach to writing gospel poetry. I think it is gospel music that has impacted my gospel poetry in various ways, such as rhythm and hopefully emotional appeal.

CR: You write poems about many different types of music, including, but not limited to, jazz and blues. Is there a spiritual component to those poems?

LDM: Oh, yes, there is a spiritual component to jazz and blues, especially jazz with the freedom to improvise and reach higher planes of expression.

CR: What relationship do you see between spirituality, music, and poetry?

LDM: The relationship I see between spirituality, music, and poetry mainly showcases freedom and expression because those elements seem to eliminate restrictions of voice if there is any at all. I feel that the divine certainly streams through all of those arts or entities and enables me to express more freely and artistically.

CR: If you could choose three of your poems that best represent this relationship, what would they be?

LDM: I hope my poems "Sunday Evening," "At the Train Stop," and "A Black Man Tells His Son the Whole Story" best represent such relationship between spirituality, music, and poetry. I wrote "Sunday Evening" in 1989 at a Ramsey Lewis instrumental concert. I tried to capture the feel of the concert. I was especially moved by Ramsey Lewis's tune "The In Crowd." Here are the opening five lines from "Sunday Evening":

> As lights glow red
> in the distant background,
> he sits at the great
> black grand.
> Fingers flutter across the keys.

One can read the poem in its entirety in my book *Geography of Jazz*. I hope the lines speak for themselves without explication.

I wrote "At the Train Stop" on Friday, November 30, 2007, riding the train to New York City. I kept looking out the window during the ride. To that end, the natural world entered the poem. The train stopped in Thelonious Monk's hometown, Rocky Mount, North Carolina. Here are the first twelve lines from "At the Train Stop," which one can also read in *Geography of Jazz*:

> I imagine the quick hand:
> Thelonious Monk waves
> at red, orange, yellow leaves
> from Raleigh to Rocky Mount.
> Alone in this seat,
> I peer out the half-window
> at the rainbow of faces
> bent toward this train

that runs to the irresistible Apple,
determine to imagine Monk
glows like Carolina sun
in cloudless blue sky.

Again, I hope the above lines can speak for themselves without explication. Moreover, I hope that the reader will bring his or her own experience and interpretation to the poem.

CR: You have written numerous poems in response to works of art. For instance, your book *The Geography of Jazz* contains many poems written about jazz performances. Another of your books, *A Temple Looming*, is comprised of portrait poems about African Americans in a series of photographs. In addition to music and photography, which other types of art do you find especially inspiring?

LDM: I find dance especially inspiring and other types of art, such as sculpture, murals, papermaking, printing, quilting, etcetera. I also find glassblowing, weaving, and tapestry inspiring.

With dance, it is because of the movement, gracefulness, rhythm, and meaning. With sculpture, it is because of the artistic development of an object from clay, glass, or metal; they all tell stories through their appearances and historic nature. Murals inspire me because of the rhythm, tone, color, patterns, and stories that they embody. I appreciate papermaking and how it leads to broadsides, pamphlets, chapbooks, etcetera, and printing inspires because of different font, styles, sizes, and colors. When it comes to quilting, I am drawn to the way the work develops into a quilt and the creative designs of the quilts. I can offer the similar comments about weaving and tapestry, though they are not different artforms. Glassblowing is inspiring because it in such a fascinating artform to watch how heat alters the shape of glass into art. All of these artforms trigger poems for me. To that end, there is no set way to writing poetry for me, especially because I like to take risks and experiment toward something new. I am delighted to answer your question about those artforms because it caused me to think deeper about my writing process.

CR: Which types of art, if any, do you find less inspiring and/or difficult to write poems about?

LDM: I am not certain about a type of art that might be less inspiring because I have written about so many types of art.

CR: When you write ekphrastic poems, how do you choose a poetic form in response to a particular artistic experience?

LDM: I am not certain that I really choose the poetic form which I might employ. I think the poetic forms choose me, except maybe haiku, tanka, haibun, and jazz poetry because I feel like they have become a part of me.

CR: Do you ever approach works of art with the intention of writing poems about them? For instance, do you listen to music planning to write about that music or see an exhibit in order to write about the exhibit? If so, how does that intention impact your experience of the art?

LDM: Yes, I have intentionally written the poems for my books *A Temple Looming* and *The Geography of Jazz*. When I first began writing those poems, I did not know that I had begun book projects. I enjoyed writing photography poems and jazz poems. When I read the poems aloud, I enjoyed how they sounded. So, I thought I might be able to write enough of those ekphrastic poems for books. When I wrote those ekphrastic poems decades ago, I did not know the word *ekphrastic*. It was not in vogue during that time. I simply wrote poems about photography, jazz, blues, and gospel.

CR: What are some examples of poems you wrote in that way?

LDM: Some examples of poems I wrote that way include "Skyward Hands"; "The Sacred Earth"; "Autumn Rain"; the poem I quoted from previously, "Sunday Evening"; and "Jazzing at the Art Gallery," among others. I wrote "Skyward Hands" on March 24, 2017, at 12:25 p.m. I attended the Senior Art Show on campus. I stood mesmerized, viewing JaQuan Blount's book sculpture. I employed my interpretation of the artwork because I thought that the sculpture's appearance somehow described itself. To that end, I did not want to do what the sculpture already did. However, I wrote "The Sacred Earth" on March 18, 2014, 2:57 p.m. I collaborated on a poetry and visual art project with my colleague Cheryl Hinton Hooks. She painted pictures of the natural world and people and photographed the natural world, including her family's farm. Her visual art inspired me to write poems. She had an exhibit, which included my poetry with her photography and paintings. She invited me to read my poetry at her opening show. And yet, "Autumn Rain" was the first poem that I wrote for our collaborative project because her painting with the same title was the first one that she lent me to write about at the time. In fact, I wrote "Autumn Rain" on December 17, 2010, at 2:28 p.m. I enjoyed our collaboration very much. Years earlier, we cotaught an interdisciplinary course, Poetry and Visual Art. To that end, we were familiar with each other's work.

CR: Do you also find yourself inspired by art that you haven't planned to write about and then decide to write a poem or poems about it?

LDM: Yes, I am usually inspired when I visit museums, concerts, and readings. I am also inspired, however, whenever I go to the beach or to the mountains. "Girl Tap Dancing" is a poem I wrote after observing Cynthia Gary tap dance at an event at Shaw University more than a quarter of a century ago. The performance was inspiring because the tap dancer's movements, rhythm, and energy were captivating; it moved me into poem mode. In short, I had to write the poem. Here is the first stanza:

> She taps, pats, clicks,
> shoes dazzling the checkered floor,
> arms whirl, whirl,
> legs cross, uncross,
> notes of the feet rise
> off tile,
> spiral toward the ceiling
> of the candlelit Ebony Club.

The entire poem can be read in *Geography of Jazz*, too. I will let the above lines speak for themselves, too. I hope the reader can get the feel of the performance from the poem.

CR: What is an example of an ekphrastic poem that surprised you either because you hadn't planned to write it or because of aspects of the poem that resulted from the experience?

LDM: The first poem "Swinging Cool" in *The Geography of Jazz* is an example of an ekphrastic poem that surprised me because I went to the jazz event to listen and enjoy. I had to write the poem. I keep a journal and ink pens on me. Lines for a poem kept tugging at me. When a poem calls, I must write.

CR: What do you find personally fulfilling or meaningful about writing ekphrastic poetry?

LDM: I try to reveal the subject in another medium from a different perspective and a different lens.

CR: How has writing ekphrastic poetry informed your other poetry, if at all?

LDM: I do not know whether ekphrastic poetry has informed my other poetry. I know I try to probe deeper than images so that there is a narrative element to my poetry. At least, I hope a narrative element is apparent in my ekphrastic poetry, too.

CR: Earlier you said, "The relationship, which I see between spirituality, music, and poetry, mainly showcases freedom and expression. I feel that the divine certainly streams through all of those arts or entities." In what ways does writing poetry about works of art enhance your experience of the divine?

LDM: I feel that writing poetry about works of art enhances my experience of the divine because I do not know where the poem will lead me. I feel that the divine guides the poem, enabling me to texturize it and hopefully capture an element of spirituality in the poem. Moreover, I feel that music helps with an element of rhythm as well as spirituality and grace.

CR: In what ways might it enhance the readers' experience of the divine?

LDM: I am not certain how my poetry might enhance the readers' experience of the divine. However, I hope my poetry can evoke a strong emotional appeal in my readers. I also hope my readers might find some connection with my poetry. In addition, I hope my poetry will strum my readers' heartstrings in some kind of way. I believe my readers feel whenever the divine deepens diction or the poem itself.

CR: What other possibilities does engaging the art of poetry to respond to different types of art potentially create?

LDM: Denotation and connotation are created when the poet engages the art of poetry in terms of responding to other types of art. I think possibilities are created by synesthesia and other elements, such as metaphors and similes. One might examine *The Geography of Jazz* for an example.

CR: Art, including poetry, can help us through painful experiences such as loss and grief. You have experienced tremendous losses in your life. How has writing poetry helped you with the grief you experienced?

LDM: I find that poetry writing and poetry reading bring solace, regarding all of the losses I have experienced in my life. I also find that poetry generates healing and comfort. Somehow, I hope to find meaning with my poetry writing. I also hope to capture segments of memories or past experiences with those whom I lose. When my daughter died, I went to the library every day or nearly every day in the last half of 2004 and much of 2005. At the library, I wrote poetry about my daughter. I employed more than twenty-five different poetic forms to write about her. I wrote enough poems for another book. Some of the poetic forms were difficult, but I taught myself how to write poetry in those poetic forms.

CR: How has reading poetry helped you?

LDM: I am not certain how reading poetry helped with the grief process because I focused more on my poetry writing. Of course, I read other poets, too. I think I mainly paid attention to the content and language. In some instances, I examined poetic forms that contained the poems so that I could try employing those poetic forms.

CR: Are there particular poems, either by you or by other poets, that you reread during difficult times?

LDM: I do not know whether I have such poems on my poem-list. I guess I have coined *poem-list*, which I hope works like the word *playlist* for songs. Thus, I have used *poem-list* for my continuous list of poems that I might read. I do like reading my poem "The Homeplace" anytime. I turn to "The Homeplace" because it depicts the way home was before all of the development and highway expansion. More importantly, it connects to my kin and a wealth of great memories. I also like reading my sestina "A Quiet Rhythm of Sleep." In addition, I like reading "Sunday Evening," because it hopefully embodies music. Then, too, I like reading from *The Open Eye, Forever Home, A Temple Looming,* and *The Geography of Jazz*. My latest book, *Long Rain*, will probably become my go to book, though *Forever Home* and *The Geography of Jazz* will always be on my reading list.

CR: You have already said that you believe the divine streams through music and poetry. Is the presence of the divine part of the reason poetry has been able to help you, both when you write it and when you read it?

LDM: Yes, I certainly think the divine helps me to write poetry and read poetry.

CR: You have addressed the loss of loved ones in poems ranging from haiku to a modified version of a bop. Is your process for selecting the right form similar to the process you described for writing ekphrastic poems, that the poetic form chooses you?

LDM: Yes, again, I think the poetic form, which I might employ, chooses me. When I write, I observe what shape the poem might take and what rhythm might be at work. I think it is like life itself; the poet must be open to changes or shifts within his or her writing process. I think I work that way. I certainly try to employ various literary elements in my poetry. At times, however, I think the ink pen just flows. I try to stay with that flow and write until I find the poem or shape the language into a poem or a genre that unfolds with figurative language into a container that becomes poetry.

CR: What do you think makes an especially effective elegy?

LDM: I think tone, subject, and diction make an especially effective elegy. I also think repetition is very effective when writing an elegy. Perhaps tone and subject are most important when writing elegies because I think they deepen the meaning. Of course, I think symbolism is important, too. Maybe the poem itself becomes living art, if possible. Maybe it captures the essence of the one whose life I celebrate. How does a poem bring comfort? Does it depend upon the reader's experience of the poem?

CR: What would you like readers to take away from your elegiac poems?

LDM: I would like readers to be able to relate to the emotional appeal and hopefully have empathy from my elegiac poems. I also hope my elegiac poems would somehow help readers with healing and that readers would be able to relate to my elegiac poems.

CR: Do you have any additional comments you would like to make about the ways in which loss and/or grief function in your poetry?

LDM: I do not have any particular comments about the ways in which loss and/or grief function in my poetry. Maybe readers will bring their own experiences to the reading of my elegiac poems. When reading my elegiac poems, I hope readers will let the poems speak to them however they might do so.

Long Rain: An Interview with Lenard D. Moore

Olga Ponomareva / 2023

From *Fireflies' Light* 26 (2022): 130–40. Reprinted by permission.

Olga Ponomareva: *Long Rain* is a collection of tanka different from your other poetry books. What enticed you to work on this book?

Lenard D. Moore: I am delighted to know that you have recognized a shift in my poetry book *Long Rain*. I have certainly tried to employ parallelism and lyricism as well as other literary elements in my tanka. I also wanted to create a sense of place in my tanka, though I strive for it in my other literary works in different poetic forms. However, I originally compiled *Long Rain* in 1994. At that time, I titled the manuscript "A Point of Light." I have held my manuscript for decades. The editor suggested that I employ another title for the book. To that end, the title was lifted from one of my tanka in the collection. The editor also suggested that I include some of my haibun in the collection. I really like that idea, especially because I had the opportunity to further my approach to the narrative element.

Ponomareva: Are these tanka biographical?

Moore: I write from the interior. Or maybe I should say I write from experience. I also write from observation. Then, too, I like innovation, especially with structure. I hope the haibun works as an introduction to each section of the book. I also hope to capture the significance of family, place, and culture. In addition, I hope to document the history and intergenerational depictions. I think my tanka embodies a sense of place and captures my hometown. I think my tanka also preserves what otherwise might become lost, such as certain traditions. I realize that there is loss, which we all experience as time progresses. Consequently, I can reread the tanka in *Long Rain* and reminisce.

Ponomareva: What qualifies as tanka?

Moore: In my approach to writing tanka, I do not think I want to pinpoint a method of writing tanka, because I like the freedom to experiment. At the same time, I strive to write tanka. In other words, I do not want to deviate from the tanka form. For example, I try to adhere to five lines. I do not adhere to a five-seven-five-seven-seven-syllable count for each line. I think a tanka should be concisely written and contain vivid imagery and symbolism. I also believe in other kinds of figurative language, such as simile and metaphor. I especially believe a tanka poem should resonate and sing. In short, I strive to employ rhythm or music in my tanka. To capture rhythm or music, I employ alliteration, assonance, consonance, euphony, and other literary elements in my tanka. However, I think understatement and irony work to strengthen tanka. Do those elements qualify to write effective tanka? I think so.

Ponomareva: Who has influenced your tanka writing through the years?

Moore: Decades ago, I read Lorraine Ellis Harr and Jane Reichhold. Several years after writing my tanka collection, I read Sanford Goldstein and Linda Jeannette Ward. It was only about a decade ago when I met Mariko Kitakubo at a gathering of poets in California. I purchased two of her tanka books, *On This Same Star* and *Cicada Forest*. I have mostly read Japanese tanka, which was translated into English. Amelia Fielden translated both Mariko Kitakubo's books into English. I have also read tanka in magazines, such as *American Tanka* and the Japanese magazine *Tanka Journal*. In addition, I have read tanka and published tanka in *Ribbons*, which is the magazine of the Tanka Society of America. Of course, I think *Dragonfly: A Quarterly of Haiku*, edited by Lorraine Ellis Harr, was the first magazine where I read tanka.

Ponomareva: The section titles of *Long Rain* give attention to the elements of earth, wind, fire, and water, but it's interesting that each part starts with a haibun which seems like a thematic guide to inform your tanka writing. Can you talk about the arrangement of each part?

Moore: Yes, you are right in regard to the arrangement of each part or section of the book. Early on, I organized the collection with the elements of earth, wind, fire, and water in mind. I wanted to do something different with my collection of tanka. I also wanted to highlight those powerful natural elements. I like the contrast of the elements. I think about how something so beautiful can be so destructive in regard to those natural elements. I also think about our connection to the earth, the oneness, and our respect for it. Now with climate change, the earth and its components are constantly altering. To that end, I wanted to document the past and present for the future. Does the title *Long Rain* allude to the terrestrial rains that fall now? What about the length of such rainfall? What if we simply contemplate the title itself?

Ponomareva: Your poems show you have a good memory of your great-grandmother. Can you share a little more about her?

Moore: Yes, I am delighted to share a little more about her. She kept busy: farming, quilting, and cooking, among other chores, such as making lye soap and raising chickens. At times, she sat on her front porch, talking to us kinfolk. She often went to church service. When kinfolk visited, she prepared great homemade meals. Many relatives came from up North. Of course, most relatives stayed South and visited, too.

Ponomareva: You are labeled a Japanese poet by Guy Davenport in his introduction, which surely means your cultural identification. How have Japanese culture and literature taken roots in your poetry?

Moore: I have appreciated Japanese culture and literature for decades. With my writing of poetry in Japanese poetic forms, I strive for cross-cultural reporting. When employing Japanese poetic forms, I strive to be observant rather than subjective. I prefer for my readers to participate in the unraveling of the poem, meaning that they bring their own experiences to it.

Ponomareva: Many poets write haiku, tanka, haibun, or others in the Japanese poetic style. Does the Japanese literary tradition make it easier to involve the reader?

Moore: Yes, I think the Japanese literary tradition opens a window to visualization, empathy, and a connection to the natural world. In other words, I feel that the Japanese literary tradition enables the reader to draw parallels with the past and present, connecting the future to the richness of experience and a sense of place. I like how the Japanese literary tradition captures what is currently happening and captures a moment.

Ponomareva: In your poems you pay special attention to a particular moment in time. Why are these moments and details more important to you than the depiction of time in general?

Moore: I hope to capture the phenomena that might be overlooked or might exhibit such beauty that cannot be ignored. Then, too, I strive to capture our ever-altering earth to preserve those moments I might be fortunate to observe. Like photography, writing has a way of capturing "aha" moments for posterity.

Ponomareva: Are you interested in photography? Has this form of visual art somehow influenced your poetry?

Moore: Yes, I am very much interested in photography. For decades, I have photographed the natural world, people, cultural arts events, and historical events. I have also photographed family members and prominent figures. In fact, my photography has been published on posters, flyers, and elsewhere. Others have also used my photography to promote their events. On another note, I have collaborated with photographers for decades: books, compact discs, and magazine and newspaper features. There also have been exhibits and readings from those collaborations, including compact discs or CDs. To that end, I have written songs or lyrics. I love songwriting.

Ponomareva: Guy Davenport in his introduction compares your observations of nature to those of Thoreau. Do you agree?

Moore: I am aware of the transcendentalist. We studied them in graduate school. I certainly have spent a lot of time exploring the land, working the land, or tending to the land, appreciating the land, and learning the land. In other words, observations of nature are so important to me. I have also been on many ginkos (haiku walks).

Ponomareva: What's the most memorable ginko for your observation of nature and where did you have that ginko?

Moore: Japan is one of the most memorable places where I have written haiku. I wrote in Tokyo and Kamakura. In fact, I wrote one hundred thirty-five haiku and one hundred thirty-five tanka during my trip to Japan in November of 2009. I was there for a week. I was invited to participate in a panel and read at the Haiku International Association Twentieth Anniversary Conference. I also took several photos of the natural world, temples, shrines, and people, including prominent haiku poets and scholars. I want to capture the sacred in my poetry.

Ponomareva: Do your poems intend to deliver a message, or do they aim at creating a feeling like a painting by impressionists?

Moore: I hope my poems do both: deliver a message and create a feeling. I believe a good poem evokes emotions within the reader. I am honored and humbled to know that you compared such a feeling in my poems to the impressionists. I am also aware of those well-known French painters. In fact, I love visual art, especially paintings.

Ponomareva: Can a painting inspire you to compose a poem?

Moore: Yes, a painting can definitely inspire me to write a poem. I have written haiku, tanka, and longer forms of poetry about paintings. I like paintings by Romare Bearden, Mary Cassatt, Cheryl Hooks, Frida Kahlo, Jacob Lawrence, Larry Lean, Beverly McIver, Norman Rockwell, and

Utagawa Toyokuni, among others. I have already collaborated with Cheryl Hooks and Larry Lean as well as other visual artists. I hope to write poetry about Beverly McIver's paintings. Maybe I will also write poetry about Utagawa Toyokuni's paintings.

Ponomareva: How is the subtitle of each part connected to the poems included in it? For instance, why is the poem about your great-grandma Fannie placed in the "earth" part and "In the Owl's Claw" in the "wind" part?

Moore: Yes, I feel that the subtitles or section titles are connected to the poems in *Long Rain*. The poem about my great-grandma Fannie is placed in the "earth" section because she owned land and worked the land. My brothers, cousins, and I worked in our great-grandma Fannie's fields. She had cornfields and peanut fields. She owned apple trees and a huge black walnut tree. Therefore, the land was significant in her life. It enabled her to can vegetables and fruit in Mason jars.

Ponomareva: And what stands behind the poems in the "wind" part?

Moore: The "wind" section opens with a haibun, depicting my observation of an owl who swoops and clenches a small bird in its claws while I am driving and listening to jazz. The sky darkens during this time. There is a sadness deepening for the small bird, though the scene embodies the natural cycle of things. I think there is something about realizing how temporary the existence of living things is, including our human existence. We, too, are part of the cycle, especially considering that we go back to dust. Therefore, I think all living things are connected in some way. The tanka in this section, however, incorporates people and the natural world. I hope this section demonstrates how everything flees like the wind. Even we are fleeting like the wind. As soon as we are born, we move closer to our departure from this world in which we live. Thus, the wind is always fleeting. No one can capture the wind. No one can stop our destiny. And yet, I hope haiku can reveal how important it is to preserve our environment. I look at haiku as ecopoetry. I look at tanka as somehow being able to strengthen the love of people, love between people, and love within people. I hope haibun can tell a compelling story about us as human beings and show deep meanings while documenting days, months, and years for future generations.

Ponomareva: Are the musical elements significant for you when composing the poems?

Moore: Yes. As you know, I have previously discussed the musical elements in an earlier answer to one of your prior questions, though I did not discuss repetition, rhyme, and anaphora. I employ those literary elements for musical effect, too.

Ponomareva: Do you use these elements intentionally, or do they come naturally as the poem unfolds?

Moore: Most times I think I am able to employ those literary elements naturally, especially because I have been writing for such a long time. There are times when I intentionally employ certain literary elements. I often can hear the music in a particular line. Rhythm is very important to me whenever I am writing.

Ponomareva: Do you often feel bonded by the natural world and is it your greatest inspiration?

Moore: No, I do not feel bonded by the natural world. I hope my poems can also help to bring about change. Maybe my poems can help us in some small way to preserve the environment. Maybe my poems can document what is happening and what was happening. I love the natural world. It certainly is my greatest inspiration, though I write poems on many subjects. I have been writing ecopoems or about the natural world for decades. As of this month, I have been writing haiku for forty years. Later this year, it will be forty years for my tanka writing, too.

Ponomareva: Congratulations! In what way can your ecopoems help preserve the natural world?

Moore: I am grateful to you for your congratulations! I hope my ecopoems can demonstrate the beauty and harmony of the natural world. To that end, I trust others would be willing to preserve the natural world. When the reader experiences my ecopoems, I hope he or she will consider his or her children and grandchildren and all the succeeding generations. I also hope my ecopoems contain a level of spirituality in them. Perhaps, we all will do our part in preserving the environment.

Ponomareva: To what extent do you prefer to be personal in your poems?

Moore: I hope my poems open up to the bigger world and not be too personal. I hope my poems resonate. I also hope the reader will return to my poems again and again. In addition, I hope my poems have emotional appeal. I plan to keep writing poems because writing is a way of life for me. Whenever the personal enters my poetry, I still try to turn my poetry into art. I think that is how a poem opens up and speaks more compellingly.

Ponomareva: How does being observant help you compose poems?

Moore: I think being observant brings an awareness, which helps me to compose poems. I am able to let go and focus so that I might craft the best poem I possibly can. Hopefully, I can encounter the moment and capture it with ease and not think about it too much. I also think being observant can help to spark imagination, which is good for poetry writing.

Ponomareva: What readers' responses do you expect for *Long Rain*?

Moore: Wow! That is a very good question. In fact, it is a tough question. I would like to continue using the word *hope* rather than *expect*. I say hope because I do not think anyone rather knows what to expect for his or her book. Of course, I know what I want for *Long Rain*, such as a wider audience. I also want *Long Rain* to lead me to another book if it is possible. When I reread *Long Rain*, maybe it will trigger poems that I wish I had written earlier, though I feel I have already had my say about the elements during that period or era when I wrote those poems.

Index

Agnew, Sharon, 6
Alexander, Francis W., 6, 31, 67
Alexander, Louis G., 61
Ammons, A. R., 29, 83, 105–6, 132

Baldwin, James, 35, 88, 92, 121
Barrax, Gerald W., 34, 37, 40, 91, 97, 99, 105, 132, 137
Bashō, Matsuo, 21, 46–47, 53, 96, 135
Brooks, Gwendolyn, 10, 21–22, 29, 34, 44, 83, 96–97, 105, 121, 130, 132, 136

Cave Canem, 67, 132, 134
Chappell, Fred, 46, 88, 96, 132
Church, L. Teresa, 66, 98, 101–2, 112

Davenport, Guy, 46, 88, 92, 96, 101, 165–66
Dove, Rita, 21, 83, 105, 121, 132, 136

Fabre, Michel, 13, 95
Frost, Robert, 30, 44, 106

Gorman, Amanda, 87–88

Harper, Michael S., 33, 82, 97, 105, 121, 132, 142
Harr, Lorraine Ellis, 5, 20, 94, 138, 164
Hayden, Robert, 61, 96, 105
Henderson, Harold G., 5, 14

Hodges, Janice W., 23, 34, 37–39, 99
Hughes, Langston, 21–22, 29, 32, 36–37, 44, 56, 82, 89, 105, 121, 130, 132, 142

Kellog, Hale, 4, 15
King, B.B., 33, 129
Knight, Etheridge, 6, 15, 31, 61, 127–28

LaSalle, Denise, 33, 129

Moore, Lenard D.: on African American aesthetics, 15–16, 97–98; African American culture, 9, 18–19, 22, 35, 115, 141; African American experience, 10, 15, 29, 35, 65, 75, 115, 141; Afrofuturism, 72, 89; Afrofuturistic haiku, 61, 89, 103, 114, 128; Black dialect/vernacular poetry, 49–50, 89; Black haiku, 70–71; Black literary renaissance, 24; bluesku/blues haiku, 16–17, 61, 103, 113–14, 135; blues poems, 4, 21–22, 25, 32–33, 47, 50, 52, 82, 84, 89, 105, 109, 128, 133–34; blues tanka, xii, 17; cadence, 48, 78; Carolina African American Writers' Collective, 4, 22–24, 34, 37–40, 58, 67, 75, 83–84, 90–91, 99, 101–2, 106, 117–18, 132, 134, 138, 154; church,

4, 22, 24, 26, 34, 37–39, 58, 75, 83, 90–91, 99, 101–2, 106, 117, 132, 134, 138, 154; diction, 12, 28, 80, 84, 115, 133, 145, 160–61; ecopoetic writing, 62; editing, 63, 65, 84, 90; ekphrastic, 47, 53, 98–100, 103, 116, 134, 137–38, 149, 157–59, 161; eye rhyme, 84, 115; form, 3, 5–6, 9, 12–20, 24, 27, 29–33, 42, 44–45, 47, 49–52, 54, 56–58, 60–62, 64–70, 75–79, 81, 83, 85, 86–87, 89, 92, 102–3, 108–9, 113–15, 119, 124–26, 127–28, 131–39, 141–42, 157–58, 160–61, 163–66; ginko, 53, 107, 120, 166; gospelku, 61, 103, 109, 114, 135; haibun, 20–21, 32, 47, 101, 109, 134, 158, 163–65, 167; haiku moment, 5, 45, 52; haiku sequence, 4, 15, 18, 52, 62–63, 68, 87, 102, 134–35; hip-hop, 24, 123; identity, 54–56; jazzku/jazz haiku, 16–17, 42, 61, 79–80, 103, 107–8, 113–14, 135; jazz poems, 4, 21–22, 26, 32, 47, 51, 105, 109, 128, 133–34, 146, 148, 158; music, 11, 14, 16, 22, 25, 29, 31, 33, 42, 47–52, 66, 70, 74–75, 77–85, 87, 90, 100, 104–8, 112–16, 122–23, 128–33, 138, 141–50, 153–61, 164, 167–68; one-line haiku, 58, 62, 94–95; one-word haiku, 62; religion, 152, 154; renga, 3, 5, 18–20, 32, 47, 138; renku, 32, 52, 65, 67, 124, 138; rhythm, 14, 16, 22, 32, 48–52, 56, 58, 63–64, 66, 69–70, 75, 77–80, 84–85, 90, 104–5, 107, 109, 112–15, 124, 128, 130, 143–44, 146, 149, 151–52, 154–57, 159–61, 164, 168; senses, 49, 57–58, 114, 125; spirituality, 153–54, 156, 159–60, 168; tanka, 3, 5, 17–19, 29–31, 45, 47, 52, 78–79, 89, 101, 107–9, 122, 131, 134–35, 154–55, 158, 163–69; three-word haiku, 62, 95

Books and chapbooks by: *All the Songs We Sing*, 75, 80, 83–84, 90–91, 101–2, 106, 153; *Desert Storm: A Brief History*, 7, 15, 17–18, 26, 41, 43, 46, 62, 75–76, 81, 87, 96, 134; *Forever Home*, 8, 12–13, 26, 36–37, 46–47, 52–54, 76, 96–98, 131, 140, 147, 161; *The Geography of Jazz*, 59, 74–75, 77, 79, 81–83, 87, 90, 103, 107–8, 111–12, 134–35, 141–43, 148, 157–61; *Long Rain*, 134, 161, 163–69; *A Million Shadows at Noon*, 24; *One Window's Light*, 58, 63–67, 90, 100–103, 115, 125; *The Open Eye*, 8, 13–14, 26, 41–42, 46, 52, 57, 66, 69, 76, 94–95, 103, 115, 161; *Poems of Love and Understanding*, 46, 74; *The Satire Project*; 60, 100, 114–16, 138; *A Temple Looming*, 24, 46–47, 52, 76, 87, 98–99, 101, 112, 127, 132, 134, 136, 157–58, 161

Poems by: "after midnight sax," 80–81; "An Album of Strong Old Men," 127; "American Jazzku," 107–8, 135; "another gospel song," 70; "Ascension: John Coltrane," 134; "At the Train Stop," 147–48, 156–57; "Autumn Rain," 158; "Azalea, Azalea," 58; "Beyond the Loon's Cry," 20; "A Black Man Tells His Son the Whole Story," 156; "a black woman," 57; "Bop: Coaching Poets," 132, 134; "A Circle of Hands," 48–49; "A Contrast of Two Lives," 98; "Double Exposure," 98; "Easter sermon," 154; "Even

Bullfrogs Get the Blues," 20; "first spring rain," 78–79; "Girl Tap Dancing," 82, 159; "Greenbriar Mall, East Point," 108–9; "The Homeplace," 13, 161; "hot afternoon," 44–45, 57–58, 125; "I'm Listening to Gospel Music," 154; "In My Memory of My Grandmother," 97; "Interlude," 146–47; "Intermission, 1956," 112, 149; "Interrogation of Harriet Tubman," 130, 134; "In the Owl's Claws," 21; "Jazzing at the Art Gallery," 158; "Jazz Suite," 148–49; "late spring sermon," 69–70; "long after sundown," 69; "Lovebeat," 150–51; "Max Roach Speaks to an Audiophile," 148; "Moses," 98; "A Note on Improvisations," 148; "the old woman" 13; "Onslow County, North Carolina," 47; "On Summer Days," 10; "on the lead singer's red robe," 155; "on the stage," 64; "A Poem for Langston Hughes," 22, 36–37; "The Poet Man/Spirit Woman," 129; "Praisesong: From Son to Mother," 54–56; "Quartet at Smoke," 111; "quiet rain," 70; "A Quiet Rhythm of Sleep," 161; "Raleigh Jazz Festival, 1986," 141; "Ray Charles Accepts Honorary Degree," 82; "red dress," 100; "Reminiscing Daddy," 131; "The Sacred Earth," 158; "September warmth," 16; "Skyward Hands," 158; "Snow in Stampede Pass," 20; "stars," 69; "Still-Life Woman," 98–99; "Stitches," 131; "Sunday Evening," 156, 158, 161; "sun plaza," 64; "Swinging Cool," 81–82, 144–45, 159; "Tanka Note," 107–8; "Telling of Tales," 10; "Twenty-Six Views of Christmas," 135; "Why Grandpa Speaks with Dignity," 10; "Woman," 98; "Yoruba," 130; "Zora Shango," 148

Moore, Maiisha, 6, 44–45, 110, 125–26, 131
Morrison, Toni, 21, 35, 88, 92, 121
Mullen, Kristi, 23
Murray, Albert, 33

Plumpp, Sterling, 32, 56, 82

Redmond, Eugene B., 53, 61, 63, 67, 72, 87, 132, 142
Reichhold, Jane, 31, 101, 164

Salaam, Kalamu ya, 6, 15, 30, 61, 103
Sanchez, Sonia, 6, 15, 30, 56, 61, 67, 73, 75–76, 102–3, 106, 127–28, 132, 136–37, 142

Taylor, Koko, 33, 129

Walker, Alice, 6, 88, 121, 137
Walker, Margaret, 88, 121–22, 136
Ward, Jerry W., Jr., 24, 72, 89, 95, 101, 132, 150
Welty, Eudora, 12
Wright, Richard, 6, 15, 21, 30–31, 61–62, 75, 83, 88, 95, 101, 121, 127–28, 137

About the Editor

Photo courtesy of the author

John Zheng is professor of English at Mississippi Valley State University and editor of *African American Haiku: Cultural Visions*; *The Other World of Richard Wright: Perspectives on His Haiku*; *Conversations with Jerry W. Ward Jr.*; *Conversations with Dana Gioia*; and *Conversations with Sterling Plumpp* and coeditor of *Conversations with Gish Jen*, all published by University Press of Mississippi.

www.ingramcontent.com/pod-product-compliance
Lightning Source LLC
Chambersburg PA
CBHW030110170426
43198CB00009B/571